GILL'S IRI

OSCAR WILDE

RICHARD PINE

GILL AND MACMILLAN

First published 1983 by
Gill and Macmillan Ltd
Goldenbridge
Dublin 8
with associated companies in
London, New York, Delhi, Hong Kong,
Johannesburg, Lagos, Melbourne,
Singapore, Tokyo

0 7171 1163 6 (paperback)
0 7171 1303 5 (hardback)

available in this series:
Michael Collins (Leon Ó Broin)
Seán O'Casey (Hugh Hunt)
C. S. Parnell (Paul Bew)
James Craig (Patrick Buckland)
James Joyce (Peter Costello)
Eamon de Valera (T. Ryle Dwyer)
Daniel O'Connell (Fergus O'Ferrall)
Theobald Wolfe Tone (Henry Boylan)
Edward Carson (A. T. Q. Stewart)
James Connolly (Ruth Dudley Edwards)
Arthur Griffith (Calton Younger)
Jonathan Swift (Bernard Tucker)
George Bernard Shaw (John O'Donovan)
Oscar Wilde (Richard Pine)
Seán Lemass (Brian Farrell)
W. B. Yeats (Augustine Martin)

The author and publisher are grateful to Hart-Davis
MacGibbon Ltd/Granada Publishing Ltd, and the Trustee
of the Estate of Vyvyan Holland for permission to
reproduce extracts from *The Letters of Oscar Wilde*, ed.
Rupert Hart-Davis (1962).

Origination by Galaxy Reproductions Ltd, Dublin
Printed in Hong Kong

Contents

For my parents

Introduction

Oscar Wilde is a difficult subject to classify or to characterise; because he does not fit into any particular critical definition or social type, he demands to be analysed as an exception: that is, on his own terms, against the social and artistic mainstream. He challenged, in his own person, the written and unwritten conventions of Victorian England, using as his weapons epigram, paradox and satire. His greatest achievement was to create his own paradox, amusing and bewildering the world as he impersonated himself. He moved consciously through controlled phases, adopting poses, creating and manipulating masks; yet who or what hid behind them? 'Try as we may,' he said, 'we cannot get behind the appearance of things to the reality. And the terrible reason may be that there is no reality in things apart from appearances.'[1]

Wilde had four phases: first *genesis*, the climb to social and artistic success, his affair with aestheticism, his self-advertisement, marriage, the difficult early years; second *hubris*, as he began to live through decadent idioms, his vanity making him reckless; third *nemesis*, his eclipse, as he was exposed, imprisoned, exiled, and deprived of position; finally a posthumous, cathartic phase, the survival of his reputation as an artist, the gathering momentum of interest in his works, the rescue of his literary estate from bankruptcy, his life retold with what Shaw called 'a healthy objectivity' (Mary Hyde 120).

Wilde claimed:

[2]

> I was one who stood in symbolic relations to the art
> and culture of my age. . . . I had realised this for
> myself at the very dawn of my manhood, and had
> forced my age to realise it afterwards. (*L* 466, 473)

He was, as Arthur Symons called him, a supreme
artist in intellectual attitudes, maintaining a calculated
discrepancy between himself and an age of which he
was both child and master,

> a man who so effectively summed up and imperson-
> ated in his life and in his writings, some of the
> vital tendencies of an epoch. (Bendz 6)

'An astonishing, impudent microcosm' (Le Gallienne
159), he pushed back the frontiers of popular drama,
forged a new style of wit, renewed the role of the
critic, defied convention, epitomised modernity.
Even though in many aspects his importance is only
minor and peripheral — such as his tenuous links with
the Celtic renaissance — he corresponded with so
many contemporary trends that he becomes that
frustrating paradox typical of his age: achieving the
status of a major figure while exhibiting all the
characteristics of a minor master. His *cause célèbre*,
his comedies and his table-talk have created a cumul-
ative, fragmented reputation which has caught the
imagination of every kind of writer from journalist
to historian.

Despite that often-quoted remark to André Gide,
'I have put all my genius into my life, and only my
talent into my work', there were few significant
concrete events in Wilde's life, from his birth in
Dublin in 1854 to his death in Paris in 1900 — in
itself an improbable odyssey. It has frequently been
said since their appearance in 1962 that Wilde's
Letters are the major source-book for his life. But

what characteristics do they disclose? Cynicism, deceit, candour, hysteria, elegance, charm, but seldom [3] real wit or more than a superficial intelligence. Nevertheless all his writings provide us with material for biographical interpretation, often in the absence of other reliable guidelines.

I have not tried to include in this little book all the known facts about Wilde, or to evaluate the merits of all the disputed incidents and *ipsissima verba* which so many others have described. I have limited my scope to the drawing of a personality, using only the facts which seem relevant and which could be corroborated, preferably by documentary evidence. This may reduce Wilde's superficial stature as a wit, but I believe it increases his authenticity as a thinker in action.

In writing this book I have become indebted to many people for their advice, assistance and encouragement: among them I am happy to acknowledge Harford Montgomery Hyde; Michael Holroyd; Rupert Croft-Cooke; Julian Symons; Monk Gibbon; Sir Rupert Hart-Davis; the late Micheál Mac Liammóir; the late T. G. Wilson; Sir Rivers Carew and Timothy Brownlow (former editors of the *Dublin Magazine*); the former and present senior partners of Parker, Garrett & Co.; J.-P. B. Ross; my oldest friend, Sebastian Garrett; William McCormack; Brian Tobin; Ninian Falkiner; Sandra Clarke; my teachers John Field, J. D. Pheiffer, Terence Brown and J. V. Rice; and the librarians of the William Andrews Clark Library (UCLA), of Duke Humphrey's Library at the Bodleian, Oxford, and of the Department of Older Printed Books, Trinity College, Dublin; also Louis and Maeve McRedmond, who united this book with its publisher; my family who thoughtfully left home so I could write it; and David Tomkin and Melanie Pine who made valuable corrections and improvements throughout.

Abbreviations

For convenience I have made abbreviated references in the text to the following works:

AC: The Artist as Critic: Critical Writings of Oscar Wilde, ed. Richard Ellmann, 1970

Bosie: Bosie: The Story of Lord Alfred Douglas, Rupert Croft-Cooke, 1963

CH: Oscar Wilde: The Critical Heritage, ed. Karl Beckson, 1970

Clark Cat.: The Library of William Andrews Clark Jr: Wilde and Wildeiana, 5 vols, ed. R. E. Cowan and W. A. Clark, 1922-31

Dulau: *A Collection of Original Manuscripts . . .,* Dulau & Co., 1928

EL: Essays and Lectures by Oscar Wilde, 1909

Hyde: *Oscar Wilde*, H. Montgomery Hyde, 1976

IR: Oscar Wilde: Interviews and Recollections, ed. E. H. Mikhail, 1979

L: The Letters of Oscar Wilde, ed. Rupert Hart-Davis 1962

Mason: *Bibliography of Oscar Wilde*, Stuart Mason [C. S. Millard] , 1914; repr. 1967

Misc.: Miscellanies by Oscar Wilde: Vol. 14 of *Collected Works*, 1908

Pearson: *Life of Oscar Wilde*, Hesketh Pearson, 1954; repr. 1966

R: Reviews by Oscar Wilde: Vol. 13 of *Collected Works*, 1908

Ross: Robert Ross, Friend of Friends, Margery Ross, 1952

Son: Son of Oscar Wilde, Vyvyan Holland, 1954, paper 1957

T: The Trials of Oscar Wilde, ed. H. Montgomery Hyde, Penguin Books, 1962; Dover Books, 1973 (same pagination)

TCV: Twentieth-Century Views: Oscar Wilde, ed. Richard Ellmann, 1969

W: Complete Works of Oscar Wilde, with an introduction by Vyvyan Holland, 1966

Other works are referred to in the text by their authors and can be found in the bibliography. References in each case have been made to the most accessible source (i.e. in the most recent edition).

1
Genesis

'Half-Civilised Blood'

> She and my father had bequeathed me a name they
> had made noble and honoured, not only in Literat-
> ure, Art, Archaeology and Science, but in the public
> history of my own country, in its evolution as a
> nation. (*L* 458)

Oscar Wilde's parents were both distinguished. William
Wilde (1815-75) a Connaught Protestant, having
studied medicine in London, Vienna and Berlin,
established from Dublin a European reputation for
discoveries in otology and ophthalmology (his classic
Aural Surgery appeared in 1853); he founded his own
hospital (the precursor of the Royal Victoria Eye and
Ear), edited the *Dublin Journal of Medical Science*,
published two topographical volumes and a collection
of folklore, and made a significant contribution (with
other scholars of his generation, such as Petrie,
O'Curry and O'Donovan) to the Celtic renaissance as
an antiquarian and archaeologist. In 1853 at the age
of thirty-eight he was appointed 'Surgeon-Oculist in
Ordinary to the Queen in Ireland', and from 1841 he
was Medical Census Commissioner responsible for
analysing the death statistics; in 1864 he was knighted
for this pioneer service. He also received the Swedish
Order of the Polar Star from the successor to King
Oscar, on whom (it is believed) he had successfully
operated for cataract.

William Wilde represented the new generation of
[6] European doctors, pioneers emerging from the dark
ages of disease and medical ignorance, where practice
was largely based on folklore such as that of the
Connaught people whom Mahaffy of Trinity called
'the most charming peasantry in Europe'; they in
their turn called Wilde *'an doctúir mór'*, the great
doctor. Wilde spoke Irish fluently and loved the
primitive exposed countryside of Connemara, where
he bought a fishing lodge on Lough Fee (Illaunroe)
and later built another at Moytura on Lough Corrib.

Jane Wilde (c. 1824-96) was born into the Wexford
family of Elgee. She had a precocious poetic temperament which, fired by the example of Thomas Davis,
brought her as a contributor of inflammatory prose
and verse under the pseudonym of 'Speranza', to
Gavan Duffy's *The Nation*: 'an early version of Maud
Gonne' (Sullivan 6). The height of her efforts was an
article 'Jacta Alea Est' in the issue of 19 July 1848
for which the editor was unsuccessfully prosecuted
for treason. In 1851 she married the rising Dr Wilde
and continued her literary career less contentiously,
translating works by Dumas, Lamartine, and
Meinhold's Gothic novel, *Sidonia the Sorceress*. Like
her husband, she also made compilations of folklore
(though hers probably utilised his leftover manuscripts). Her verse, eighteenth-century in inspiration,
admired by her contemporaries, was eclipsed by the
modern development of Anglo-Irish literature. Wilde in
later life claimed that Speranza ranked intellectually
with Elizabeth Barrett Browning (*L* 496) and that her
pen 'set the young Irelanders in a blaze' (*L* 80).[2]

Both Jane Elgee and William Wilde were well connected in the Anglo-Irish middle classes. William's
father was a doctor, his uncle and both his brothers
clergymen. Jane, although she is said to have had more
purely Irish blood than her husband, also had more

'establishment' figures in her family, including landed gentry such as the Ormsby family. A cousin, Robert [7] McClure, was knighted for his part in the exploration of the North-West Passage. She was also related to the Rev. Charles Maturin, the curious author of the Gothic novel *Melmoth the Wanderer* which influenced her younger son.[3]

The Wildes married in 1851. Their first son, William, was born in 1852, their second, Oscar, in 1854 on 16 October. (A daughter, Isola, born in 1858, died in 1867.) As these first-generation Dubliners prospered they moved from Great Brunswick (now Pearse) Street to 21 Westland Row (where the boys were born) and then to a grand mansion at No 1 Merrion Square, in a part of the city that had once been the home of the aristocracy but that had for the last thirty years become increasingly the target of the professional middle classes.

Willie and Oscar Wilde were familiar with both the prestiged echelons of the upper middle class and the rural environment of the West of Ireland so dear to their father. They also had an early revelation of social double values, not exclusive to Dublin. In the year of Oscar's birth Dr Wilde, who was a promiscuous, highly sexed man, began an affair with Mary Travers, daughter of a Dublin professor. She bore him a child, but, unlike the mothers of his several other illegitimate children, she did not fade out of his life. Ten years later she publicised the affair, prosecuted the incautious Lady Wilde for libel, in an action where Sir William, at the height of his career, refused to give evidence for his wife, earning the censure 'a pithecoid person of extraordinary sensuality and cowardice'. Miss Travers won a farthing damages. At the ages of ten and twelve respectively, Oscar and Willie witnessed the family name being brought into disrepute through a court case and a sex scandal.

The Wilde children had an unorthodox upbringing.
[8] As Rowan Hamilton said of the parents:

> He is a man of great activity and considerable cultivation. . . . She is undoubtedly a genius herself . . . almost amusingly fearless and original, and *vows* . . . that she likes to make a *sensation*. (White, 123)

The Dublin-born cartoonist Harry Furniss said Speranza had 'the appearance and air of a tragedy queen' (Furniss 1).

One of Wilde's schoolfriends recalled that

> He wanted to be the hero of a *cause célèbre* and to go down to posterity as the defendant in such a case as *Regina v. Wilde*. (Brasol 31)

— and at Oxford he declared: 'Somehow or other I'll be famous, and if not famous I'll be notorious.' (*IR* 5) With Sir William's increasing self-isolation after the Travers scandal, Speranza had greater control of the children. After her second son's birth she wrote to Rowan Hamilton: 'He is to be called Oscar Fingal Wilde. Is not that grand, misty and Ossianic?' (Broad 23) For the poetess to call her heroic child after the son of Ossian is understandable, but it has also been suggested that he was named after the King of Sweden, who, it is said, became a — presumably proxy — godfather. But an indigenous reason is more likely: Oscar was an extremely popular name in the West of Ireland in the mid-nineteenth century and, as the revival of interest in the bardic tradition developed, came into general use in Ireland, as evidenced in the names of patriots such as Osgur Breathnach and Oscar Traynor. (It is perhaps surprising that by contrast the Wildes' elder son was called purely by family names: William Charles Kingsbury.)

Although Dublin's middle-class hierarchy was extraordinarily Protestant — there were few city-centre

Catholic churches, for example, and only two of William Wilde's close friends, Aubrey de Vere and John Gilbert, were Catholic — its Protestantism was 'Irish' rather than 'Anglican', and its culture in the mid-nineteenth century was indigenous. It also tended, as in the case of the Wilde family, to be closely connected with the countryside, which, even in nearby Co. Wicklow, where they holidayed, was alive to primitive culture; this contact made them strongly conscious of fantasy, both in popular superstition and in the writings of their friends, such as Sheridan Le Fanu.

Oscar Wilde had a deep love of the Irish countryside. Holidaying at Illaunroe, he admired its setting on the edge of Europe, a peninsula covered with wild fuchsia (perhaps accounting for its name, the 'red island'), amid some of the most barren terrain in Europe, 'this wild and mountainous country' (L 54). After a college examination he wrote: 'I am resting here in the mountains — great peace and quiet everywhere', as if he were in Switzerland or Macedonia — an imaginative realm at his disposal and to which he felt a substantial emotional commitment. He had what Yeats called 'that half-civilised blood in his veins'. He saw in the peasant approach to the Catholic faith the valid survival of pagan rituals in the folk-life of the Irish countryside (something which three other Irish Protestants, Yeats, Synge and Lady Gregory, were to introduce directly into the repertoire of the National Theatre at the turn of the century). Wilde, for example, remained (at least sentimentally) convinced of the existence of the *bean sídhe* (banshee, or woman of the fairies) whom, he claimed, he heard when a death was imminent.

As a result of his upbringing, Wilde provides many interesting examples of those provincial turns of phrase known collectively as the 'Anglo-Irish language'. In his letters he referred to football as 'a tedious game to be always playing' (L 592) and in an essay he says

'not to be always worrying' (*W* 1086), translations
[10] from an Irish colloquial idiom which characterise
Anglo-Irish usage. In the original version of *The
Importance of Being Earnest* he wrote that one character 'goes long walks', which an editor studiously
converted to 'goes *on* long walks'; and his Duchess
of Padua exclaims: 'Sure it is the guilty / Who being
very wretched need love most.' (*W* 616; *L* 136) A
further example of Irish translation was a remark
made to Vincent O'Sullivan in about 1894: 'I think
he must be there *yet*' (i.e. *still*: O'Sullivan 76). When
Wilde was preparing *An Ideal Husband* for publication
in 1899 he asked Robert Ross to 'see that the "wills"
and the "shalls" are not too Hibernian' (*L* 789); and.
as I shall show, he and Shaw started a 'Celtic school'
of plays in the full consciousness of their acute
relationship to the London playgoers and manage-
ments: in fact Wilde's Irishness was a key factor in his
career, involving both something exotic and something
naive in his character, as far as his audience, the
English, were to see him.

2
'More Rhyme than Reason'

In 1865 Oscar joined Willie at Portora Royal School
near Enniskillen, Co Fermanagh. Little is recorded of
his schooldays, except a general recollection that he
was imaginative, studious and uninterested in games.
Further supposition would be wrong.

In 1871 Wilde was admitted to Trinity College,
Dublin, having achieved second place overall in the
entrance examination. He had won an entrance
scholarship from Portora and in 1873 won a foundation scholarship. In the following year he won the
Berkeley Gold Medal for a classical essay. Most of the
winners of the Berkeley Medal in those years went

on to fellowships and professorships or, like Edward
Carson, to high positions at the Bar and Bench. [11]

Wilde made a point of appearing indolent and care-
free, but in fact he knew the value of hard work and
very much wanted to shine in his parents' estimation.
His mother continued all her life to support and
encourage him, and wrote, on publication of one of
his earliest poems: 'The poem *looks* and reads *perfect*
— musical and poetic — the evident spirit of a *poet
natural* in it.' (White 235)

Apparently Wilde's college rooms were 'exceedingly
grimy and ill-kept' (*IR* 1). A college contemporary
remembered him ten years later as a clumsy but well-
meaning, generous type; he 'hardly ever made a step
he didn't knock something over' (*IR* 2). Many years
later his 'elephantine gait' was still remarkable. There
is also evidence of Wilde's physical strength and courage in resisting class bullies. He joked with his college
comrades that he and his mother had established 'a
Society for the Suppression of Virtue'. His precocious
talents were encouraged in those areas which interested
his parents and tutors — the composition of sentimental verse, the classics and Greek philosophy.

The main influence in his eighteenth, nineteenth and
twentieth years was his tutor, the young Professor of
Ancient History, John Pentland Mahaffy (1839-1919) 'a
man of high and distinguished culture . . . one to whom
I owe so much personally . . . my first and best teacher
. . . the scholar who showed me how to love Greek
things' (*L* 338). Mahaffy drew close parallels between
Ireland and Greece, for example calling the Rock of
Cashel 'the Irish Acropolis', just as Sir William Wilde
had called the Boyne megalithic tombs a 'Royal Necro-
polis' comparable to that of Memphis. In his written
work he often drew parallels between the Greek and
Irish peasants and their environment, and Wilde later
criticised Mahaffy for his 'attempts to treat the Hellenic

world as "Tipperary writ large"' (*AC* 80). No doubt
Mahaffy was the father of Wilde's remark to Yeats
that the Irish were the greatest talkers since the Greeks.

Mahaffy was a socialite with a highly developed
sense of the importance and effectiveness of conversational ability, particularly at table, which he passed
on to Oscar Wilde. For Mahaffy conversation was 'the
social result of Western civilisation, beginning with
the Greeks' (*Principles* 1), 'a perpetual intellectual
feast' (p. 3). It was often said that Wilde's conversation
was so brilliant that it must have been written down,
polished and studied intensely, rather than extempore.
Mahaffy insisted that wit must be spontaneous, that
'anyone suspected of coming out with prepared smart
things is received by the company with ridicule', but
allowed that conversational skill required a good
memory, perhaps aided by some shorthand notes
(pp 84-5). The qualities necessary for good conversation, according to Mahaffy, were a sweet tone of
voice, with absence of local accent and of tricks or
catchwords; knowledge and quickness; modesty,
simplicity, unselfishness, sympathy and tact. Wilde,
like his tutor, lacked many of these.

Mahaffy's other sphere of influence was in teaching
Wilde the value of Hellenism. In this he was a vigorous
and highly prejudiced teacher, being violently opposed
to both Roman classical culture and the influence of
the Roman Catholic Church.

In 1874 Mahaffy published *Social Life in Greece*,
acknowledging the assistance of 'my old pupil Mr
Oscar Wilde' for his 'improvements and corrections
all through the book'. Mahaffy's was the first frank
discussion of Greek homosexuality, 'the peculiar
delight and excitement felt by the Greeks in the
society of handsome youths ... the same sort of
agreeable zest which young men of our time feel in
the company of young ladies' (*Social Life* 305).

Mahaffy was a fair exponent: 'But such an entertainment as the modern ball would have appeared to the [13] old Greek profoundly immoral and shocking, just as we are apt to regard his attachments as contrary to all reason and sense of propriety. There is no field of enquiry where we are so dogmatic in our social prejudices.' In the second edition in 1875 Mahaffy replaced this section with a discussion of the Greek response to female beauty, 'which will be suited to all classes of readers; so that the book in its present form can be made of general use for schools and family reading'. Homosexuality belonged to a social and literary underworld, defying the 'social prejudices' of mid-Victorian Britain. In Wilde's case it became steadily stronger until it dominated his consciousness and his character. This was a steady process, rather than a state which suddenly materialised in early middle age.

It is not clear why Wilde left Trinity without a degree in order to enter Magdalen College, Oxford, with an entrance scholarship (a 'demy') on 17 October 1874, the day after his twentieth birthday. There was no reason why the Wildes should want to send their younger son to Oxford; Mahaffy himself frowned on the export of young Irish talent, but in Oscar Wilde's case he may have felt that his pupil was temperamentally unsuited for a Trinity fellowship, or that Irish society was too small to contain an obviously large and precocious talent. However, Lady Wilde was pleased: 'Oscar is now a scholar at Oxford, and resides there in the very focus of intellect.' (Hyde 17)

'The two great turning-points of my life were when my father sent me to Oxford, and when society sent me to prison,' Wilde wrote from the latter place. (*L* 469) He remembered his time at Oxford as

days of lyrical ardour and of studious sonnet-making; . . . delightful days, in which, I am glad to say, there was far more rhyme than reason. (*R* 538)

[14] Among his college friends his conversation and manners were frank. David Hunter Blair, a Catholic convert who became Abbot of Fort Augustus, recalled Wilde's 'large features lit up by intelligence, sparkling eyes and broad, cheerful smile' (*IR* 3), and another friend, recognising the love of pose, the desire for self-realisation, the egotism, remembered:

> How brilliant and radiant he could be! How playful and charming! How his moods varied, and how he revelled in inconsistency! The whim of the moment he openly acknowledged as his dictator. (*IR* 12).

Another Oxford contemporary recalled that his conversation consisted of

> a flood of paradoxes, untenable propositions, quaint comments . . . preposterous theories . . . His talk charmed because it was plainly the utterance of a gay and engaging and keen spirit. (*IR* 23)

It was this gift, and his hard-necked self-advertisement, which bought his way to success in London.

At the same time, as an Irishman he was an outsider at Oxford; furthermore, he was two or three years older than the average undergraduate — a significant difference. Other aspects of his background combined to set him apart from his fellows: he was familiar with viceregal society; he came from a milieu which, while it did not formally encourage eccentricity, certainly condoned it and had drawn more flexible social boundaries than those prevailing in England; he was much closer to a peasant culture than most of his university colleagues, and in his first epiphany outside his native country he found a new status for the *seanchaí* (story-teller), whose artistry conferred social position in the hierarchical Gaelic society which persisted within contemporary Ireland. A modern metamorphosis of the role of the *seanchaí*, from the classical niche to the hybrid platform, is evident in Wilde's interest in the scholar-citizen type which he outlined in *The Picture of Dorian Gray* —

> to combine something of the real culture of the scholar with the grace and distinction and perfect manner of a citizen of the world (*W* 103)

— an aristocrat among the artists, the super-*seanchaí*, a man of action, typified for Wilde by George Nathanial Curzon (1859-1925), his contemporary at Oxford, later member of parliament, Viceroy of India, Foreign Secretary and marquess.

Wilde's university career in Dublin and Oxford (1872-79), coincided with the development of the debate on the relationship of art to life. While this had its most spectacular expression in the 1890s, the seeds were sown mainly in the 1860s and 1870s.[4]

The main topics of discussion at Oxford — the 'home of lost causes and forsaken ideals and unpopular names and impossible loyalties', as Arnold called it (Brasol 56) — were belief and identity: religion, the relationship of life and art, the role of criticism (both aesthetic and historical). Wilde entered fully and earnestly into these discussions, particularly when they concerned religion and art.

Even thirty years after Newman's conversion to Roman Catholicism Oxford was still coming to terms with its consequences. Partly excited by the genre of Pre-Raphaelite art, and despite the vigorous opposition of most college heads and dons, large numbers of undergraduates attended St Aloysius' Catholic Church (where during Wilde's years Gerard Manley Hopkins was assistant priest) and became Roman Catholics.

Wilde's own views on the 'Newman debate' were that 'His higher emotions revolted against Rome but

... he was swept on by logic to accept it as the only
[16] rational form of Christianity.' 'His life', Wilde judged,
'is a terrible tragedy.' (*L* 20) The fine balance between
logic and emotion was a factor in his development
both as an 'aesthete' and as 'a man of the world'.
During these Oxford years he was almost continually
in doubts and suffering from anxieties as, away from
home, he tried to find his real identity. He was
immediately attracted to Rome, perhaps as a reaction
to the anti-Roman atmosphere of Merrion Square and
Trinity, but vacillated. He was

> caught in the fowler's snare, in the wiles of the
> Scarlet Woman — I may go over in the vac [Easter
> 1877]. I have dreams ... of the holy sacrament in
> a new Church, and of a quiet and peace afterwards
> in my soul. I need not say though, that I shift
> with every breath of thought, and am weaker and
> more self-deceiving than ever. (*L* 31)

Four months earlier he had been admitted to the
Scottish Masonic rite in the Oxford University Chapter
— presumably for social reasons; like Dorian Gray, 'he
never fell into the error of arresting his intellectual
development by any formal acceptance of creed or
system' (*W* 106).

At Oxford Wilde characteristically announced his
rejection of logic:

> I confess not to be a worshipper at the Temple of
> Reason. I think man's reason the most misleading
> and thwarting guide that the sun looks upon, except
> perhaps the reason of woman. (*L* 20)

This coincided with his introduction to the Oxford
don Walter Pater (1839-94) whose message, enshrined
in his *Studies in the History of the Renaissance* ('the
book which has had such a strange influence over my
life': *L* 471), was to become a form of gospel for the
next generation:

Art comes to you proposing frankly to bring nothing but the highest quality to your moments [17] as they pass, and simply for those moments' sake.

Pater saw

a counted number of pulses only . . . of a variegated dramatic life. How shall we pass most swiftly from point to point, and be present at the point where the greatest number of vital forces unite in that purest energy? To burn always with this hard, gem-like flame, to maintain this ecstasy, is success in life. (*Renaissance* 251)

Inclined to self-interest, thrown onto his own resources by his comparatively alien life in Oxford, Wilde developed both a critical instinct and a poetic faculty. In a creative way he contributed to the development of English criticism; the process can be crudely summarised as follows:

(1) 'The function of criticism [is] to see the object as in itself it really is.' (Matthew Arnold, 1864)
(2) 'In aesthetic criticism the first step towards seeing one's object as it really is, is to know one's own impression as it really is.' (Walter Pater, 1873)
(3) 'The primary aim of the critic is to see the object as in itself it really is not.' (Oscar Wilde, 1891)

Where Pater spoke of a 'multiplied consciousness', Wilde conceived of a 'multiplied personality', a series of attitudes and a series of masks, with which to encounter reality. He began (in an unsuccessful Oxford prize essay on 'The Rise of Historical Criticism') to emphasise the individuality of the critic-historian, a stance which he developed almost obsessively throughout his critical writings. Following Pater he realised that there was no point in doing anything unless one could *be* oneself. He attached considerable importance

to Emerson's phrase 'Nothing is more rare in any man
[18] than an act of his own', on which he commented:

> Most people are other people, their thoughts are
> someone else's opinions, their lives a mimicry, their
> passions a quotation. (*L* 479)

Believing that everyone is capable of realising himself
by living life to the full, he developed an epicurean
creed which was first respectably classical, then toler-
ably humorous and, finally, offensively modern. On a
personal level he saw himself as 'a born antinomian . . .
one of those who are made for exceptions, not laws'
(*L* 468).

Meanwhile he continued his undergraduate career,
as one visitor to his rooms recorded, 'with his long-
haired head full of nonsense regarding the Church of
Rome. His rooms filled with photographs of the Pope
and Cardinal Manning.' (*L* 14) Wilde's family whole-
heartedly disapproved of this behaviour, which must
have seemed a betrayal of class, education and politics:
'My father rejoiced at my winning a scholarship to
Oxford where I should not be exposed to pernicious
influences, and now my best friend turns out to be a
Papist.' (Broad 35-6) It may have been at his parents'
instigation that in 1879 Mahaffy, travelling to Greece,
carried Wilde off from an Italian holiday, saying: 'I will
make an honest pagan of you' and writing to his wife:

> We have taken Oscar Wilde with us, who has of
> course come round under the influence of the
> moment from Papacy to Paganism, but what his
> Jesuit friends will say, who supplied the money to
> land him at Rome [i.e. Hunter Blair], it is not hard
> to guess. I think it is a fair case of cheating the
> Devil. (Stanford and McDowell 41-2)

As a result of his being late back at Oxford, he was
fined and sent down for the remainder of that term.

'I was sent down from Oxford for being the first undergraduate to visit Olympia,' he later told Charles [19] Ricketts. (*L* 36)

Wilde's conduct was never wholly orthodox, but he conformed in many details to the regular undergraduate pattern, writing with an adolescent banter, appealing to his mother to send 'the genial £5' (*L* 11), always sending the conventional good and respectful wishes to the mothers and sisters of his correspondents, being a dutiful weekend guest; but it is also very clear from his Oxford letters — written to very close and sympathetic friends — that he was aware of homosexual behaviour within his own college and was prepared to condone and speculate about it. At the same time he was paying attention to pretty girls, who seem to have been attracted to him.

Wilde may simply have been experimenting with his confused and immature emotions. He refers to one friend as 'a pleasant affectionate boy', and another ('my greatest chum') as *'psychological'*, i.e. homosexual (*L* 32). At the same time he was writing teasingly: 'I am just going out to bring an exquisitely pretty girl to afternoon service at the Cathedral' (*L* 24), and he was obviously strongly attracted to beauty in the female form. One mother, finding her daughter upon his knee, allegedly remonstrated with him: 'The thing was neither right nor manly nor gentlemanlike.... So low and vulgar was it, that I could not have believed anyone of refined mind capable of such a thing. . . . I would rather see her dead than bold, free or immodest.' (A. J. A. Symons 162) He was engaged unofficially to a Dublin girl, Florence Balcombe, described by Du Maurier as one of the three most beautiful women in England. She later married Bram Stoker, secretary to Irving and creator of *Dracula*, who it has been suggested brought funds to Wilde in his last days in Paris.

A further sign of indecision is the florid, effusive
[20] prose style which continued throughout his twenties
and in fact persisted until he reached a plateau of style
during his years as a critic. A histrionic touch became
evident when he discussed friendship, art or religion:
'This is an era in my life, a crisis. I wish I could look
into the seeds of time and see what is coming.' (L 34)
He often abandoned himself to the unknown, exposing
a weakness of judgement which placed him in the way
of difficulties from which he could not extract himself.

Many of Wilde's later flirtatious letters were of the
'gushing' type ('I hope the laurels are not too thick
across your brows for me to kiss your eyelids': L 277),
suggesting an emotional immaturity which is also
apparent in the 'purple' passages of his essays and
Dorian Gray. There is also an hysterical element, a
superficial response to an emotional stimulus, in which
'everything is valued in superlatives'.[5] It was easy for
a highly charged personality such as Wilde's to yield
to every temptation, taking Pater's epicureanism to
its conclusion:

> I wanted to eat of the fruit of all the trees in the
> garden of the world. . . . I was going out into the
> world with that passion in my soul. . . . I don't re-
> gret for a single moment having lived for pleasure. . . .
> There was no pleasure I did not experience. . . .
> The other half of the garden had its secrets for me
> also. (L 475)

Wilde's other activity at this time was writing poetry.
During his holiday in Italy he had visited Ravenna,
which was the subject for the 1878 Newdigate Prize
poem, which he won (previous winners included
Ruskin and Arnold). He recited the poem in the
Sheldonian Theatre on 26 June 1878, and it was then
published by the university (Mason 301), Wilde
himself purchasing 150 copies.

Both at Trinity and at Magdalen Wilde displayed the capacity for hard work, often reading, with the [21] advantage of a very retentive memory, late into the night: 'I suppose one ought to be a Gibeonite, a 'wood-hewer and water-drawer of Literature' in order to make one's First safe.' (*L* 28) He took a first in Mods, but in his third year his work slackened and he failed to win the Ireland Scholarship. In his fourth year he borrowed a friend's notes on philosophy (mainly Plato) and asked for advice on examination technique: 'I am reading hard for a Fourth in Greats. (How are the mighty fallen!!)' (*L* 48) These gloomy speculations were proved to be unfounded when he succeeded in obtaining a 'double first'.

He began to develop a sense of self-importance, regarding his visits home as those of a celebrity ('The Dublin people all think I am a Fellow of Magdalen, and so listen to all I say with great attention': *L* 29) and skilfully exaggerating his real importance: on a later visit (1882) he told a girl-friend he was 'dining with the Fellows of Trinity', a grand way of saying that he had been invited on the top table at Commons, the college evening meal.

For the second time Wilde relinquished a university career. Having put behind him the chance of a Trinity fellowship, which would have elevated him among the company of Mahaffy, Tyrrell and Lecky — and perhaps, if he became interested in politics, given him a safe university seat — he also declined to sit the Magdalen fellowship examinations (although after his first class degree his demyship was renewed for a fifth year in 1879 for this purpose). He seemed to prefer to find his own way in London, in a sense affirming his interest in the modern and its future rather than in the past and its interpretation. Despite his academic excellence, he certainly seems to have been temperamentally unsuited to a university career as a

'dried-up don' (*IR* 5). It is an indication of his elusive-
[22] ness as a person that one biographer has said that
Wilde 'came to Oxford as a brilliant Irishman. He left
it an Oxonian' (A. J. A. Symons 157), while another
has declared: 'Never did Oxford University turn out a
less typical Oxonian.' (Pearson 26)

As he left Oxford he visited the Oratory Church in
London to consult Father Sebastian Bowden about
becoming a Catholic. Bowden wrote:

> As a Catholic you would find yourself a new man
> in the order of nature as of grace. I mean that you
> would put from you all that is affected and unreal,
> and a thing unworthy of your better self, and live a
> life full of the deepest interests of a man who feels
> that he has a soul to save and but a few fleeting
> hours in which to save it.

Bowden had succeeded in analysing the characteristics
which Wilde had developed at Oxford: affectation, a
detachment from concrete issues, and 'a thing unworthy', i.e. a tendency, perhaps no more than
intellectual, towards homosexuality. His appeal was a
direct counter-claim to Pater: where Pater saw 'a
counted number of pulses only', Bowden talked of a
limited time in which to save a soul.

It is certain, however, that under the influence of
both Pater and Mahaffy, Wilde went into the world
convinced like Pater's Marius the Epicurean that it
held 'many voices it would be a moral weakness not
to listen to'. However, Wilde's basic characteristic
remained an undeveloped childishness, sometimes
ingenuous, sometimes petulant, sometimes hysterical,
a childishness uncontaminated and unrestrained by
tact, discretion or inhibition. Years later Lord Alfred
Douglas insisted that

> Unless you understand that Oscar is an Irishman
> through and through you will never get an idea of

what his real nature is. In many ways he is as simple
and innocent as a child. (*Bosie* 93) [23]

3
Tea and Beauties

Wilde arrived in London in 1879 as a self-styled 'Professor of Aesthetics'. It was a brave move, although
he had gained much confidence among English society
from his university contacts; with some help from
Ruskin and the Duchess of Westminster (sister of his
homosexual friend Lord Ronald Sutherland-Gower)
and a natural flair for self-advertisement common
among Oxford graduates from Shelley and Byron to
Tynan and Frost, he gradually achieved invitations to
artistic, aristocratic and bourgeois houses. 'We live in
an age of inordinate personal ambition,' Wilde wrote,
'and I am determined that the world shall understand
me.' (*L* 146)

There was little to exercise Wilde's 'immeasurable
ambition' (Pearson 64). His father had at his death
left some unfinished work which Wilde expected to
complete; 'It is a great responsibility,' he wrote, 'I
will not be idle about it' (*L* 20) — but his sense of
duty appears to have been short-lived, for the task
was eventually undertaken by his mother. He discussed
a project to translate Herodotus and Euripides for
Macmillans, but nothing came of it, nor of his desire
to translate Flaubert's *La Tentation de St Antoine*,
nor of a project to adapt Verdi's *Luisa Miller* for the
fashionable Polish actress Helena Modjeska. He was
little known outside the university, and had published
only a few poems and minor art criticism (in the course
of which he had said of Whistler's 'The Falling Rocket',
in a Ruskinian vein, that one looks at it 'for about as
long as one looks at a real rocket, that is, for some-
what less than a quarter of a minute': *Misc.* 18). He

also had the dubious distinction of the Newdigate
[24] Prize — but, as W. S. Gilbert said, 'I understand that
some young man wins this prize every year.' (*IR* 33)

He told the editor of the *Dublin University Magazine*
that 'I intend to take up the critic's life' (*L* 39) and
moved permanently, with his mother and brother, to
London — 'the focus of light, progress and intellect'
Speranza called it (White 241) — with that intention,
his first professional pose being one of his most
successful. He shortly afterwards explained his
departure from Ireland as an artistic one:

> I live in London for its artistic life and opportun-
> ities. There is no lack of culture in Ireland but it is
> nearly all absorbed in politics. Had I remained there
> my career would have been a political one. (*IR* 63)

At the same time he tried to get a respectable
position as a schools inspector, which, as in Arnold's
case, was compatible with a critic's life, giving more
emphasis to the established and classical than the daring
and modern: 'Rents being as extinct in Ireland as the
dodo or moly, I want to get a position with an assured
income.' (*L* 63) Wilde spent three years in London,
adopting a Bohemian lifestyle in company with Frank
Miles, an artist friend, first in rooms off the Strand,
then in Tite Street, Chelsea. They often entertained in
'this untidy and romantic house' at a social event called
'tea and beauties', as well as holding evening parties
which were attended by actresses like 'Lily' Langtry,
Ellen Terry and Sarah Bernhardt and titled ladies such
as Lady Desart and the Countess of Lonsdale.

Many of these subsequently recalled their impressions, and it is important in reading these to distinguish
those who saw in Wilde merely a repellent physical
presence, confirming in retrospect their view of his
character; those who found that his personal charm,
or the fascination of his speech, overcame their initial

repulsion; and those who recorded their immediate contemporaneous impressions, such as 'Vernon Lee' (i.e. Violet Paget), who reported:

> He talked a sort of lyrico-sarcastic maudlin cultschah for half an hour. But I think the creature is clever and that a good half of his absurdities are mere laughing at people. The English don't see that. (Gunn 78)

Another who stands halfway between those repulsed and those attracted by Wilde is William Rothenstein, who recalled

> a huge and rather fleshy figure, floridly dressed. . . . His hands were fat and useless looking. . . . But before he left I was charmed by his conversation, and his looks were forgotten. . . . I, who was in some ways more innocent than most youth of my age, saw little to be afraid of in this new friendship. There was certainly something florid, almost vulgar in his appearance, and his manners were emphasised. . . . But he had an extraordinary illuminating intellect. (Rothenstein 86-7)

When in January 1882 he arrived in America the *New York World* observed his 'broad shoulders and long arms, indicating considerable strength' and announced that 'A peculiarity of Mr Wilde's face is the exaggerated oval of the Italian face carried into the English type of countenance and tipped with a long sharp chin. It does not, however, impress one as being a strong face.' Later that year the *Rochester Democrat* called it 'emphatically the face of a dreamer, intelligent and refined, but not the face that would inspire confidence in earnestness of purpose and vigour of execution' (*IR* 59), while the *Toronto Evening News* summed it up as 'a fine face of effeminate cast'. Others later recorded (see *IR* 127, 137, 257, 339, 371) his 'brilliance', his 'genial and kindly' nature, his 'witty impertinence'.

'Affected in manner, yes,' said Rothenstein, 'but it [26] was an affectation which, so far as his conversation was concerned allowed the fullest possible play to his brilliant faculties.' One of those faculties was invention, and another pastiche. Sir Henry Newbolt in 1932 recalled an evening in 1887 when Wilde spoke of the lesser-known Elizabethan and Jacobean dramatists:

> His quotations seemed to bear out all that he claimed for them and I noted the names that I might study them at my leisure. But when I searched the plays afterwards I found not a word of any of the lines. . . . The imitations were so perfect and so striking in themselves as to be worthy of the forged names he appended to them. (*Pearson* 176)

It is also clear that at least from his Oxford days Wilde had a very considerable conversational charm. As Alfred Douglas attested:

> The most remarkable and arresting thing about Wilde was that without any apparent effort he exercised a sort of enchantment which transmuted the ordinary things of life and invested them with strangeness and glamour. The popular idea of him as a man who fired off epigrams at intervals and was continually being amusing is quite inadequate to explain his charm and fascination. He had a way of looking at life, and a point of view which were magical in their effect. (*Without Apology* 75)

At the time of his trial (1895) the newspaper caricatures were mostly aggressive portraits of a callous, vice-ridden sybarite, and this image seems to have been projected onto the memories of his contemporaries. However, examination of the portrait photographs of Wilde from 1880 up to 1895 reveal none of the 'bestial', 'coarse' or 'repulsive' features which retrospective prejudice recalls; it is true that the photographs do not show the bad teeth which everyone agrees he had from an early age, and which in conversation, particularly in laughter, he covered with his hand. It would be fair to say that there is an accurate consensus in describing Wilde's appearance as sensuous and effeminate, and in detecting looseness in his face and a tendency to grossness in his general frame. Although he was physically unattractive, his charm and bonhomie carried off his grosser defects: largesse of charm compensated for an excess of vulgarity.

*　　*　　*

Wilde went to London in a certain crusading spirit. In 'De Profundis' he wrote of Christ, obviously with himself in mind:

His chief war was against the Philistines.... Philistinism was the note of the age and community in which he lived. In their heavy inaccessibility to ideas, their dull respectability, their tedious orthodoxy, their worship of vulgar success, their intense preoccupation with the gross materialistic side of life, and their ridiculous estimate of themselves and their importance, the [Jews] of Jerusalem in Christ's day [were] the exact counterpart of the British Philistine of our own. (L 485-6)

He wrote a play, *Vera, or the Nihilists*, which shows this crusading spirit:

... to express ... that Titan cry of the peoples for liberty, which in the Europe of our day is threatening thrones, and making governments unstable. ... But it is a play not of politics but of passion. (L 148-9)

He knew nothing as yet of stagecraft and had to admit that 'The only reason, to speak honestly, that the play is as good an acting play as it is [which it is

not], is that I took every actor's suggestion I could
[28] get.' (*L* 104) Wilde had no currency as a dramatist —
Vera was melodrama intended as social comment and
as such fell between two stools, whereas poetry offered
him a more immediate entree to the attention of a
society concerned with 'aesthetics' — the relation of
art to life.

There was no 'aesthetic movement' in the sense of
a perceivable group with a conscious policy of mani-
festo — unlike the Pre-Raphaelites or indeed the
Dadaists — but it was evident in the spirit of renewal,
for example in house decoration, dress reform and a
poetic renaissance, all of which Wilde successfully
appropriated and all of which were vigorously caricatured by the popular press.

'Aestheticism' had a long and confused pedigree;
Arthur Symons called it 'a beautiful farce'. Pre-
Raphaelitism and the crafts movement encouraged
by William Morris on the practical level, Pater and
Ruskin on the academic, were its most obvious sources.
Its motto, first expressed by Théophile Gautier, was
'art for art's sake'. An 'aesthete' was probably more
concrete in the caricatures by Du Maurier in *Punch*
than in flesh and blood, but, as Sir Michael Levey says,
Gilbert and Sullivan's *Patience* 'could only be effective
if there was a trend to satirise' (Levey 183). The trend
was towards the greater introduction of art into life —
a sense of artistic values, a practical use of art products
(e.g. in house decoration) and an appreciation of
poetry and the visual arts. Satire was in fact widespread and directed towards the more outrageous
forms of behaviour encouraged by the 'aesthetic
movement', sometimes exemplified by Wilde himself
in his more camp moments.

The authors of *Patience* did not in fact wish to mock
the sincere expression of art for art's sake but directed
their satire against a 'clique of professors of ultra-

refinement, who preach the gospel of morbid languor and sickly sensuousness . . . unmanly oddities', while *Punch* complained that 'aestheticism' had come to mean 'an effeminate, invertebrate, sensuous sentiment-ally-Christian, but thoroughly Pagan taste in literature and art, which delights in the idea of the Great God Pan'.[6]

Wilde had been in London for two years before Du Maurier's cartoons or any of the texts in *Punch* were discernibly directed towards him, so his impact on the satirists was not immediate. During 1881, however, he became well known as a result of their attentions; he gave them a useful focus for their caricature, particularly because his own effeminacy appeared languid and sensuous. Du Maurier stated clearly that neither of his prize aesthetes (Postlethwaite and Maudle) was based on Wilde (*Pall Mall Gazette*, 19 May 1894), but Wilde was throughout his career sus-ceptible to caricature and was readily associated in the popular imagination with other satires such as Lambert Streyke in *The Colonel* by *Punch*'s editor Francis Burnand. As a result of both Du Maurier's and *Patience*'s jibes, for example, Gerard Manley Hopkins called him 'Oscar the utterly utter' (Winwar 65).

During 1879 and 1880 Wilde and Miles were milk-ing the aesthetic craze for all the notoriety it afforded them; they were supported by 'puffs' from Willie Wilde, who had become a successful gossip columnist on Edmund Yates's *Time* and *The World* as well as drama critic for *Vanity Fair*.[7] They directed much of their artistic energy towards Lily Langtry: 'I with my pencil and Oscar with his pen, will make Lily the Joconde and the Laura of this century.' The 'Jersey Lily' also allowed Wilde to advise her on dress, and 'he advised me to improve my mind by attending . . . lectures on Greek art at the British Museum' (*IR* 263). For a short time Wilde acted as her amanuensis, and it was rumoured that he was among her numerous lovers.

[30]   In August 1880 Wilde received some genuine attention in *The Biograph and Review* (which also carried
three of his poems and announced that 'At the coming
Christmas Mr Wilde purposes bringing out a blank
verse tragedy in four acts, some essays on Greek art,
and a collection of poems'). The biography — responsible for later biographical errors in stating his year of
birth as 1856 — no doubt at Wilde's own suggestion
— referred to him as:

> A believer in the religion of beauty ... the off-
> spring of a fervid emotional race. ... In him the
> strong emotional tendency of the Irish nature which
> with most of the race feeds personal feeling alone
> becomes through intellectual development an
> ardour for art and its glories.

Similarly in 1882 Walter Hamilton in *The Aesthetic
Movement in England* defended Wilde against satire
and called for a serious assessment, seeing Wilde as a
latter-day Pre-Raphaelite.

Much of Wilde's time was occupied in writing
poetry. *Time* and *The World* published several of his
poems in 1879, 1880 and 1881. He had sent poems
to Gladstone appealing for support, but received little
encouragement, although he acknowledged him as
'the one English Statesman who has understood us
[the Irish], who has sympathised with us, whom we
claim now as our leader' (*L* 237). In 1881, very
conscious of 'not having set the world quite on fire
as yet' (*L* 61), he decided to collect all his work
together, coming to the usual arrangement for unknown, uncommercial, ambitious young poets,
whereby Wilde paid the publishing costs and the
publisher, David Bogue, took a 10 per cent commission on sales.[8] Wilde gave away many copies of
Poems, soliciting testimonials from, among others,

Robert Browning, Matthew Arnold and Swinburne (and in the following year from the literati of Paris).

Wilde's prefatory poem, 'Hélas!' (*W* 709) was very revealing:

> To drift with every passion till my soul / Is a stringed lute on which all winds can play, / Is it for this that I have given away / Mine ancient wisdom, and austere control? . . . / Surely there was a time I might have trod / The sunlit heights, and from life's dissonance / Struck one clear chord to reach the ears of God: / Is that time dead? lo! with a little rod / I did but touch the honey of romance − / And must I lose a soul's inheritance?[9]

This questioning, already remorseful poem pinpoints Wilde's dilemma. Wilde never succeeded as a poet, but *Poems* does enable us to confirm his strong awareness of his homosexuality, expressed in the poetic genre called 'Uranian',[10] which in addition to describing homosexual emotions, celebrates the relationship of older men with boys, a further development of which was the class distinction between upper- or middle-class men and working-class boys, later so important in Wilde's case.

Poems contains many pieces unconnected with love, particularly sonnets on liberty, the theatre, and devotional themes, across a Pre-Raphaelite canvas, but especially interesting is a section devoted to the classical and pastoral subjects which Uranians employed to conceal the identity of their 'modern' loves. For example, in 'Endymion':

> You cannot choose but know my love / For he a shepherd's crook doth bear, / And he is soft as any dove / And brown and curly is his hair . . . / Where is my own true lover gone, Where are the lips vermilion? . . . / Ah! Thou hast young Endymion, / Thou hast the lips that should be kissed! (*W* 750)

'Charmides' (*W* 753-70), a 'morbid' account of a
[32] young man's love for a statue, also explores the theme
of narcissism, the disillusioned self-love that encour-
ages 'a strange and secret smile':

> It is Narcissus, his own paramour, / Those are the
> fond and crimson lips no woman can allure.

Another Uranian evasion was substitution, writing
a piece about a boy and then making the subject into
a girl. Wilde's most obvious substitution was a poem
originally entitled 'Wasted Days', first published in
the TCD magazine *Kottabos* in 1877:

> A fair slim boy not made for this world's pain, /
> With hair of gold thick clustering round his ears . . . /
> Pale cheeks whereon no kiss has left a stain, / Red
> under-lip drawn in for fear of Love, / And white
> throat whiter than the breast of dove — / Alas! alas!
> if all should be in vain . . . The boy still dreams;
> nor knows that night is night, / And that in the
> night-time no man gathers fruit. (*W* 732)

In *Poems* the verse is retitled 'Madonna Mia', the 'fair
slim boy' becomes a 'lily-girl', and the whole suggestion
of impossible seduction is turned into one of hopeless
worship:

> Yet, though my lips shall praise her without cease, /
> Even to kiss her feet I am not bold.

As a result of most Uranian passion being unrequit-
ed — at least in verse — the poet often expresses his
inability to find a refuge. Wilde, like Melmoth, found
himself condemned to 'travel wearily / And bruise my
feet, and drink wine salt with tears' (*W* 731) — the
typical fate of the outcast, ridden with guilt and
'shame'.

The sense of 'sin', which was most acute among
Uranian writers, appears in *Poems* ('My white soul /

First kissed the mouth of sin'), and in 'San Miniato' (*W* 725) Wilde writes:

> O listen ere the searching sun / Show to the world my sin and shame

— an extremely early use in this context of 'shame'. 'Shame', in Uranian verse, was accompanied by 'anguish' and 'remorse'. In 'The Burden of Itys' (*W* 739) Wilde unequivocally expresses the torture of homosexual love:

> . . . memories of Salmacis / Who is not boy nor girl and yet is both, / Fed by two fires and unsatisfied / Through their excess, each passion being loth / For love's own sake to leave the other's side / Yet killing love by staying.

Salmacis was a fountain which made effeminate all who drank of it: Hermaphrodite changed his sex there. The final poem, 'Flower of Love' (*W* 802-3), suggests that Wilde may have had one 'platonic' love affair at Oxford: in an amplification of 'Hélas!' he tells his beloved:

> I blame you not, for mine the fault was . . . / From the wildness of my wasted passion I had struck a better, clearer song . . . / I have made my choice, have loved my poems, and, though my youth is gone in wasted days, / I have found the lover's crown of myrtle better than the poet's crown of bays.

The critics were not impressed with *Poems*. The *Saturday Review* condemned its 'imitation, insincerity and bad taste'; the *Spectator* called its author 'a clever man, with a host of sensuous pictures in his mind, sometimes passing into pure sensuality . . . who has an infinite contempt for his readers, and thinks he can take them in'; Oscar Browning, a well-known academic and literary homosexual, whom Wilde

had asked to review the book, recognising that Wilde
had been 'marked out as representing the newest
development of academical aestheticism', advised him,
through the columns of *The Academy*, to keep 'his
passion, his sense of beauty, his gift of language and
metre' and to 'apply to himself the stern self-discipline
necessary for excellence' (*CH* 40).

Wilde simply took advantage of aestheticism – he
'prevailed upon' his age (Chamberlin xi), and *Poems*,
as the *Athenaeum* observed, 'may be regarded as the
evangel of a new creed. From other gospels it differs
in coming after, instead of before, the cult it seeks
to establish.' (*CH* 33) While most Uranians and
inverts, like Pater, Symonds and Gosse, insisted on
caution, Wilde insisted on advertisement. Society
acknowledged it in the satirical columns. In 1881, for
example, Du Maurier's aesthetic caricature Maudle, who
had been in existence since 1880, adopted some of
Wilde's physical appearance and was cartooned saying:

> *Maudle:* How *consummately lovely* your son is,
> Mrs Brown.
> *Mrs Brown:* What? He's a *nice manly* boy, if you
> mean *that*, Mr Maudle.

In 1883 the *Illustrated Sporting and Dramatic News*
cartooned Wilde in convict dress. This has been
mentioned as an ironic forecast of his fate; but if it
was intended as a joke at the expense of Wilde's sexual
inclinations, it was very sinister. In 1883 the law under
which Wilde was imprisoned (for gross indecency) had
not yet been introduced, and the only homosexual
offence on the statute book was sodomy, to which it
must be assumed this cartoon referred.[11]

The greatest satire, however, was Gilbert's and
Sullivan's *Patience*, which D'Oyly Carte presented at
London's Opera Comique on 23 April 1881. *Patience*'s
aesthetes, Bunthorne and Grosvenor, are not expressly

based on Wilde but are directed towards the excesses of aestheticism – what Du Maurier had called 'Nincompoopiana'.

In the gossip column of *The World* Willie announced that his brother had been invited to lecture in America – a statement completely without foundation. However, *Patience* opened in New York in late 1881; Carte realised that it needed a 'curtain-raiser', and he arranged for Wilde to be invited to lecture there. Eventually the tour began in January 1882. Wilde certainly kept his part of the bargain, agreeing with one interviewer that he was the model for Maudle, and donning 'aesthetic' costume (kneebreeches, velvet jacket, etc.) whenever necessary and caricaturing himself in aesthetic postures. His American adventure made him both the butt and the publicist of the 'aesthetic craze' (*The Colonel* also followed *Patience* to America) and also gave him the opportunity to formulate his personal gospel, to prove that he had 'something to say'.

4
'I Have Something to Say to the American People'

I have something to say to the American people, something that I know will be the beginning of a great movement here. . . . I should be very disappointed if when I left for Europe, I had not influenced in however slight a way the growing spirit of art in this country, very disappointed if I had not out of the many who listen to me made one person love beautiful things a little more. (*L* 88-91)

During his American tour all Wilde's early poses – scholar, poet, apostle – crystallise. Now aged twenty-seven, he was in an extremely precarious position. He had no secure family roots, a very slender reputation as an aesthetic artist, little income and few friends.

He took Carte's offer because it held the prospect of
[36] immediate work, new experience and future status,
even though it must have seemed to him as if his
sincere beliefs about art would be subject to ridicule.

The need to produce a text concentrated Wilde's
own thoughts. He was obliged to explain very clearly
to his audience what he meant by the 'aesthetic
movement', describing the English renaissance as

> a sort of new breath of the spirit of man like the
> great Italian Renaissance of the fifteenth century,
> in its desire for a more gracious and comely way of
> life, its passion for physical beauty, its exclusive
> attention to form, its seeking for new subjects of
> poetry, new forms of art, new intellectual and
> imaginative enjoyments. (*EL* 111-12)

> It is really from the union of Hellenism, in its
> breadth, its sanity of purpose, its calm possession
> of beauty, with the adventive, the intensified
> individualism, the passionate colour of the romantic
> spirit, that springs the art of the nineteenth cen-
> tury in England. (*EL* 112).

He had no hesitation in claiming the leadership of
the movement: 'I would from them create an artistic
movement that might change, as it has changed, the
face of England. So I sought them out — leader they
would call me.' Despite elocution coaching by the
actor Hermann Vezin, his first lecture at Chickering
Hall, New York, on 9 January 1882 was, like the next
few, delivered in a dull monotone, but his delivery
improved as he gained confidence in this new form of
expression, although he rarely departed from his prepared script. While he adopted an exaggerated artistic
pose, he appeared sincere in delivering his five lectures:
'The English Renaissance in Art', 'House Decoration'
(the two most common), 'Dress Reform', 'Art and
the Handicraftsman' and 'The Irish Poets of '48'.

In America Wilde discovered his emphasis on the momentary and the exceptional, his own response to Pater's theory of 'fleeting moments', while his marriage of the classical and romantic spirits gave rise to his own special accent on modernity, the justification for individualism. In America too we can see him consciously moving away from Pre-Raphaelitism towards an 'increased sense of the absolutely satisfying value of beautiful workmanship, this recognition of the primary importance of the sensuous element in art, the love of art for art's sake' (*Misc.* 31). He characterised himself as a Paterian, a man of thoughts rather than action, one 'who seeks for experience itself and not for the fruits of experience . . . who must burn always with one of the passions of this fiery coloured world. . . . For art comes to one professing primarily to give nothing but the highest quality to one's moments, and for those moments' sake,' he told his American audiences, almost in Pater's own words. (*EL* 151-2) He told the *Daily Examiner* (San Francisco, 27 March 1882): 'A poem is well written or badly written. In art there should be no reference to a standard of good or evil.'

As far as understanding all this was concerned, he claimed that 'If you ask nine tenths of the British public what is the meaning of the word aesthetics they will tell you it is the French for affectation or the German for a dado' (*EL* 119); and he described satire as 'the homage which mediocrity pays to genius' — obviously summing up Gilbert's and Sullivan's relationship to himself.

On arrival in New York he had been 'taken up' by Mrs Frank Leslie, proprietor of the *Illustrated Newspaper*, in which she reported: 'Oscar Wilde is almost niched and pedestalled by society.' (She was subsequently, and briefly, married to Willie Wilde.) Wilde had a letter of introduction from Sir Edward Burne-

Jones to Charles Eliot Norton ('He has much bright-
ened this last of my declining years': *L* 123) and
was in fact lionised by American society. He met
Oliver Wendell Holmes, Walt Whitman and Julia Ward
Howe, and was looked after by Dion Boucicault, the
Irish dramatist, who was living in America at that time.

Henry James, having met him in New York, called
him 'an unclean beast . . . a fatuous cad' (Edel I 649).
Boucicault wrote to Mrs George Lewis, wife of the
London solicitor who specialised in sex cases, both
heterosexual and homosexual, and who seems to have
asked him to keep an eye on Wilde:

> I do wish I could make him less Sybarite – less
> Epicurean. . . . There is a future for him here, but
> he *wants management*. Carte thought he had got
> hold of a popular fool. When he found that he was
> astride of a live animal instead of a wooden toy, he
> was taken aback. (*L* 92-3)

Reports of his activities seem, however, to have
caused some annoyance among the aesthetes in
England, presumably due to his self-assumed position
of leadership. Swinburne is quoted as saying: 'I
thought he seemed a harmless young nobody and had
no notion that he was the sort of man to play the
mountebank as he seems to have been doing.' (*L* 100)
Wilde boasted to Mrs Lewis that 'As regards my
practical influence I have succeeded beyond my
wildest hope. In every city they start schools of
decorative art after my visit, and set on foot public
museums, getting my advice. . . . The artists treat me
like a young god.' (*L* 99) From Griggsville (whose
citizens he advised: 'Begin by changing the name of
your town') he told her: 'At present the style here is
Griggsville Rococo and there are also traces of
"archaic Griggsville", but in a few days the Griggsville
Renaissance will blossom. It will have an exquisite

bloom for a week and then ... become "debased Griggsville and the Griggsville Decadence".' (*L* 103)

Wilde's tour took him from New York to Philadelphia, Washington, Boston, and then to many cities of the United States as well as some smaller towns — and some of the mining settlements of Colorado: 'I read them passages from the auto-biography of Benvenuto Cellini and they seemed delighted,' he subsequently told British audiences. 'I was reproved by my hearers for not having brought him with me. I explained that he had been dead for some little time, which elicited the inquiry "who shot him?".' (*AC* 9-10) Only once did he experience any personal threat, and this too among the trigger-happy miners of Colorado. 'I was told that if I went there they would be sure to shoot me or my travelling manager. I told them', said Wilde, appropriating a story his father used to tell (*L* 547) of the absentee Earl of Clanricarde, 'that nothing they could do to my manager would intimidate me.'

In St Louis he was hailed as 'Speranza's Gifted Son', in New Orleans as 'the Apostle of Modern Art', in Topeka, Kansas, as 'the Prince of the Aesthetes', and adulation was equally mixed with fascination; but in many places he was mocked, partly as the representative of Bunthorne and partly because of his own languid, indolent appearance. Few of the ordinary newspaper reporters would have agreed with the *New York Daily Tribune* that 'Oscar Wilde's message is one which is really wanted in the United States' (11 June 1882), or with the *Montreal Daily Star* that accusations of affectation had been offensive. Most, like the Charleston *News and Courier*, regarded him as 'an enlarged and magnified lah-da-dah young man [who] spoke with the "don't-you-know" yawp of the day' (*IR* 98).

In his lecture 'The Irish Poets of '48', delivered in

San Francisco, Wilde expressed the acute relationship
of 'Celtic-Irish' and 'British' traditions:

> The poetic genius of the Celtic race never flags or
> wearies . . . and indeed I do not know anything
> more wonderful, or more characteristic of the
> Celtic genius, than the quick artistic spirit in which
> we adapted ourselves to the English tongue. The
> Saxon took our lands from us and left them
> desolate — we took their language and added new
> beauties to it.

After six months' work Wilde's net receipts exceeded £1,000 (his fee ranged from £40 to £100 depending on the location), and he hoped to travel to Japan to study art there, and to lecture for Carte in Australia, where *Patience* was to be produced. A volume he proposed to Whistler would have been one of the curiosities of literature: 'When will you come to Japan? Fancy the book, I to write it, you to illustrate it, we would be rich.' (*L* 121) But Carte prevailed on him to undertake further American lectures in much smaller places for much smaller fees. Eventually his savings eroded, and he stayed inexpensively for two months with friends in New York. Here he unsuccessfully solicited a position as European correspondent for the publisher J. M. Stoddart, discussed the production of *Vera* with Marie Prescott after Carte had refused to produce it, and negotiated a contract with Mary Anderson for his next play, *The Duchess of Padua.* He sailed for Liverpool at the end of 1882.

5
The House Beautiful

'Enough money to give myself an autumn at Venice, a winter in Rome and a spring in Athens' (*L* 91) was what Wilde hoped for from the American tour. Eventually he netted enough, after a brief stop-over in London, to take him to Paris for a few weeks in the spring of 1883. He failed to make a great impact there. He met Daudet, Hugo, Edmond de Goncourt, Paul Bourget, Zola, Verlaine, Degas, Pissarro and Jacques-Émile Blanche, but was not generally very highly regarded. Zola was openly rude to him, Hugo slept through the audience he granted, and Goncourt recorded in his diary: 'this person of ambiguous sex, the language of a ham-actor, and phony stories'.

To a new acquaintance, Robert Sherard, he announced: 'The Oscar of the first period is dead! We are now concerned with the Oscar of the second period.' He abandoned his 'aesthetic' costume and dressed conventionally, if floridly, having his hair curled and waved: 'Society must be amazed, and my Neronian coiffure has amazed it.' (L 147) One lady noticed the difference between the Oscar of the first and second periods: 'He is grown enormously fat with a huge face and tight curls all over his head, not at all the aesthete he used to look.' (Hyde 88) However, like earlier dandies, Disraeli and Bulwer (Lytton) for example, he succeeded in conveying an overriding impression of *style*.

At the same time he began to work hard again. He was invited to Italy by a friend of his mother, but declined: 'At present I am deep in literary work and cannot stir from my little rooms on the Seine till I have finished two plays. . . . The drama seems to me to be the meeting of art and life.' (L 146) One play, soon dispatched to Mary Anderson, was *The Duchess of Padua*, 'Op. II'. There is no record of the other, but this is the first indication of Wilde's sincere commitment as a playwright.

Sending the manuscript of *The Duchess of Padua* to America, Wilde called it 'the masterpiece of all my literary work, the *chef-d'oeuvre* of my youth' (L 136) and only much later admitted that it was 'unfit for publication – the only one of my works that comes under that category' (*L* 757). He instructed Mary Anderson as to its merit and potential, conceiving the play as a vehicle for 'intense emotion with a background of intellectual speculation' (*L* 136) – as with *Vera*, a recipe for disaster.

His youthful enthusiasm for *The Duchess of Padua* and his self-confidence must have caused Mary Anderson to smile – 'That I can create for you a part which will give your genius every scope, your passion every outlet, and your beauty every power, I am well assured.' Despite the difference in their ages – Wilde was nearly twenty-eight, she only twenty-three – she was the more mature, and she was cautious too, her stage career having made her wise beyond her years. She can hardly have taken seriously his earnest and pompous observation that 'Perhaps for both of us it may mean the climacteric of our lives.' (*L* 127) She rejected *The Duchess of Padua,* a decision which shocked and disappointed Wilde.[12]

He returned to America, however, for the première of *Vera*, which was produced in New York on 20 August 1883 and was a failure, although the critics' views demonstrated their perennial disparity: the *New York Tribune* called it 'unreal, long-winded, wearisome', the *New York Herald* 'long-drawn dramatic rot', while the *New York Mirror* acclaimed it as 'the noblest contribution to its literature the stage has received in many years'. The play ran for one week and had a brief tour later that year. Wilde chose to forget his first flop.

In the meantime the agent who had arranged his American tour had signed him up to lecture throughout Britain. He had joked to Mrs Lewis: 'I promise you never, never, to lecture in England, *not even* at dinner' (*L* 103), but with his social and professional ambitions he obviously did not mean it.

In addition to his aesthetic discourses, he was now able to give his 'Impressions of America', the first delivery being in the Prince's Hall, Piccadilly, on 9 July 1883. He continued to lecture on both topics throughout 1884 and 1885, 'civilising the provinces by my remarkable lectures' (*L* 155). He was in the lucky position of being able to pioneer his views of the American people, and in so doing he probably originated the 'American joke'; for example:

> So infinitesimal did I find the knowledge of Art west of the Rocky Mountains, that an art patron . . . actually sued the railroad company for damages because the plaster cast of Venus de Milo, which he had imported from Paris, had been delivered minus the arms. And what is more surprising still, he gained his case and the damages. (*AC* 10)

He also lectured to the students of the Royal Academy, having gleaned some ideas in conversation with Whistler, who later accused Wilde of purloining his theories on art, describing the consequent rupture of the friendship in *The Gentle Art of Making Enemies*. However, Wilde took little from Whistler, as the lecture embodied his own rapidly developing theories on creativity ('What you as painters have to paint is not things as they are, but things as they are not: *EL* 209), and while he may have had in mind Whistler's own work — pictures which he had mocked as early as 1877 — as examples of non-representational painting, he may as easily have been influenced by the French Impressionists. His friendship with Whistler (another alien in London), which really amounted to a sparring partnership, was unlikely in any case to survive their combined egotism.

Dress sense was one area in which Wilde, like the other aesthetes, seriously attempted to achieve reform.

He wrote and lectured extensively on the need for
[44] more gracefulness and common sense in the female
costume. As for men, Wilde suggested that the
costume of 1840 would enliven evening dress through
the reintroduction of colour in men's coats, which
was otherwise available only in the choice of button-
hole. For women, not only appearance but also
hygiene and convenience were considerations:

> As long as the lower garments are suspended from
> the hips, a corset is an absolute necessity; the mis-
> take lies in not suspending all garments from the
> shoulders. . . . The modern high-heeled boot is, in
> fact, merely the clog of the time of Henry VI, with
> the front left out, and its inevitable effect is to
> throw the body forward, to shorten the steps, and
> consequently to produce that want of grace which
> always follows want of freedom. . . . One of the
> chief faults of modern dress is that it is composed
> of far too many articles of clothing, most of which
> are of the wrong substance. (L 161-3)

In the course of his tours Wilde visited Dublin,
where he spoke at the Gaiety Theatre on 22 and 23
November. The *Irish Times* (23 November 1883)
records him announcing: 'I have not the slightest
reverence for anything in existence except for the
Eternal Being, the memory of great men, and the
principle of beauty.' An old family friend, Constance
Lloyd, who was visiting relations there (she also now
lived in London) attended his lectures and invited
him to tea at her grandmother's house in Ely Place.
She thought him 'decidedly extra affected, I suppose
partly from nervousness', but 'he made himself very
pleasant'. Three days later, to the surprise of everyone including herself, she announced their engage-
ment (L 152-3). Writing to Lily Langtry, Wilde
described his fiancée as 'a grave, slight, violet-eyed

little Artemis, with great coils of heavy brown hair which makes her flower-like head droop like a blossom, and wonderful ivory hands' (*L* 154). Shaw said of her: 'She was not a pretty woman, and never can have been; but she was not ugly: her appearance simply calls for no comment' (Mary Hyde 120). Willie announced her in *The World* as 'the lady whom he has chosen to be the châtelaine of the House Beautiful'. Lady Wilde, who had had Constance Lloyd in mind for some years as a prospective daughter-in-law, was delighted: 'I would like you to have a small house in London, and live the literary life, and teach Constance to correct proofs, and eventually to go into Parliament.' (*Hyde* 92)

Constance was well connected: her father and grandfather had been QCs, and a great-uncle succeeded Edward Carson as Solicitor-General for Ireland, 1892-95, and later became Lord Hemphill.

'When I have you for my husband', Constance wrote to Wilde, 'I will hold you fast with chains of love and devotion so that you will never leave me or love anyone so long as I can love and comfort you.' They were married on 29 May 1884. The wedding was 'aesthetic'; Whistler telegrammed: 'Am delayed. Don't wait.' Wilde mis-stated his age as twenty-eight (he was twenty-nine). The honeymoon was spent in Paris. Wilde's enthusiasm for the marriage was conventional; he extolled his bride and busied himself with the preparation of the House Beautiful, a few doors down Tite Street from his bachelor rooms. It is impossible to judge what he expected from marriage. From the ambivalent attitude he had already displayed towards women and men, and from his subsequent history, it is tempting to look on his marriage as one of convenience. There was a basic difference between them: according to Pearson, she told Wilde: ' I hold that there is no perfect art without perfect morality,

while you say they are distinct and separate things.'
[46] (Pearson 111) But it was important to be settled after
several years of unproductive drifting; it was essential
to have a basic income, which Constance's dowry
provided; it was perhaps advantageous to use
matrimony as a blind for his other attachments (after
his own downfall many homosexuals took this step).
Yeats saw Wilde's wife and children as an artificiality,
'some deliberate artistic composition', as if the
acquisition of a family had been a phase through
which he had decided to pass, the role of husband
and father a mask he found it convenient to adopt.
He may have actually wanted a respectable domesticity and a family, which for a time he seems to have
enjoyed, the births of his sons, Cyril in 1885 and
Vyvyan in 1886, giving him great pleasure. As
Vyvyan (1886-1967) recalled:

> He had so much of the child in his own nature that
> he delighted in playing our games . . . caring nothing
> for his usually immaculate appearance. Cyril once
> asked him why he had tears in his eyes when he
> told us the story of *The Selfish Giant* and he
> replied that really beautiful things always made
> him cry. (*Son* 44-5)

He gave them copies of his favourite children's
authors: Verne's *Five Weeks in a Balloon*, Kipling's
The Jungle Book and Stevenson's *Treasure Island*.
When they went to the seaside for holidays he displayed his skill in building sand-castles, sailing and
fishing; he could also mend the children's toys.

Certainly Wilde did not intend to devote himself
exclusively to his wife; in this he was no different to
the conventional Victorian husband whose social life
was divided between home and club, and whose
morality may have been equally bifurcated. One of
the best explanations of the marriage came from

Wilde's disciple Richard Le Gallienne, who thought Constance 'a pretty young woman of the innocent Kate Greenaway type':

> They seemed very happy together, though it was impossible not to predict suffering for a woman so simple and domestic mated with a mind so searching and so perverse and a character so self-indulgent. It was hard to see where two such different natures could find a meeting place. (*IR* 391)

Their new house was beautifully decorated. Wilde was very conscious of the need to live according to his professional status, to practise what he preached, and every available penny was invested in No. 16 Tite Street. All the doors were replaced by curtains, and in most rooms the furniture was kept to a minimum. The decoration and rebuilding was carried out under the supervision of E. W. Godwin, Ellen Terry's architect lover and the father of Gordon Craig.

Constance anticipated the need to supplement her unearned income, perhaps by going on the stage, but Wilde's lecturing, although gruelling, together with his regular anonymous reviewing in the *Pall Mall Gazette* from 1884, made this unnecessary. (During Willie's holidays in 1884 he also temporarily took over the drama criticism of *Vanity Fair*.) Wilde once more tried for a schools inspectorship, this time through George Curzon. He was apprehensive lest the administrator 'may take the popular idea of me as a real idler' (*L* 178). He failed to get the job, as he did a third time in 1886, when Mahaffy was his sponsor. His last visit to Ireland was to lecture in Dublin on 5 and 6 January 1885, when the *Irish Times* (6 January) commented that 'Like Grosvenor in "Patience" he has grown stouter since we last saw him, but his peculiarities of manner are unchanged.'

As a reviewer for the *Pall Mall Gazette* Wilde wrote

on all and sundry: minor poets and novelists, translations of the classics, and works in which, for one reason or another, he had an interest; Whitman, Symonds, Swinburne, Pater, Wilfred Scawen Blunt and Andrew Lang; Froude's *The Two Chiefs of Dunboy*; lectures by Morris, Whistler and Walter Crane. He was a caustic and occasionally brutal reviewer. He had little sympathy with anything which simply repeated successful formulae favoured by the public. On a work by several authors he commented: 'It has taken four people to write it, and even to read it requires assistance' (*R* 98); of a religious volume: 'It is a thoroughly well-intentioned book and eminently suitable for invalids.' (*R* 132) A rare pun arose when he said of a work referring to cheese: 'The style is at times so monstrous and so realistic that the author should be called the Gorgon-Zola of literature.' (*AC* 85) He described Knight's *Life of Rossetti* as 'just the sort of biography Guildenstern might have written of Hamlet' (*AC* 49) and accurately if surprisingly said of Mahaffy's *Principles of the Art of Conversation*: 'If Mr Mahaffy would only write as he talks, his book would be much pleasanter reading.' (*R* 247) However, he greeted the début of W. B. Yeats in 1889 with *Fairy and Folk Tales of the Irish Peasantry*: 'Mr Yeats has a very quick instinct in finding out the best and most beautiful things' (*AC* 130), and later the same year he hailed Yeats's *The Wanderings of Oisin* as 'full of promise. . . . He is essentially Celtic, and his verse, at the best, is Celtic also.' (*AC* 150) When he met Yeats he compared his recitation of Irish legends with the story-telling of Homer. Wilde also greeted a volume from Edward Carpenter with the evangelical announcement 'Socialism . . . welcomes many and multiform natures. She rejects none and has room for all.' (*R* 425) On 'what not to read' Wilde divided books into three categories:

books to read — Cicero, Suetonius, Vasari, Cellini, Marco Polo; books to re-read — Plato and Keats, 'in the sphere of poetry the masters not the minstrels, in the sphere of philosophy the seers not the savants'; and books not to read at all — 'all John Stuart Mill except the Essay on Liberty, all Voltaire's plays ... all argumentative books, and all books that try to prove anything' (*AC* 27-9). In similar vein he once listed his dislikes as 'the dreary classical Renaissance that gave us Petrarch, and Raphael's frescoes, and Palladian architecture, and formal French tragedy, and St Paul's Cathedral, and Pope's poetry, and everything that is made from without and by dead rules' (*L* 482).

His distinction in journalism prompted Cassell's publishing house to approach him in 1887. Since November 1886 they had published *Lady's World* without much success; they now asked Wilde to associate himself with re-launching it. He looked at the offer in a businesslike manner, showing clearly that he had a feeling for the likely market and the shape that the paper should take: 'The *Lady's World* should be made the recognised organ for the expression of women's opinions on all subjects of literature, art, and modern life, and yet it should be a magazine that men could read with pleasure, and consider it a privilege to contribute to.' (*L* 195) At first he called himself a 'literary adviser' and only acknowledged the editorship at the end of the summer of 1887. He put a great deal of effort into the new magazine, retitled *Woman's World*, taking advice from some of his society contacts such as Mrs Jeune (later Lady St Helier), who intended to help him in securing contributions from royalty and the aristocracy.[13] Speranza and Constance contributed, and Wilde himself wrote 'Literary Notes' which were completely different in character to his iconoclastic pieces in the *Pall Mall Gazette*. Was Wilde writing tongue-in-cheek when he greeted the products of authoresses as 'pleasant', 'delightful', 'charming', [50] 'most interesting'? Eventually Wilde lost interest in the project in mid-1889. Cassells pointed out how little he attended the office, where he had begun as a regular worker, and with mutual relief they parted company.

Wilde was extending his interests in other directions, and there were signs that he might become financially independent. In 1888 Nutt published *The Happy Prince and other tales*. [14] (In 1889 Constance also published an illustrated children's book.) He was also developing his critical writing, but in the fifteen years since he left Ireland Wilde had achieved little. Having become almost respectable, he lacked some of the glamour and notoriety he had gained as a young Oxford graduate. He was a member of the Albemarle Club; at the turn of the decade he joined the Lyric and New Travellers clubs; he was elected a Fellow of the Society of Authors in 1887; only the Savile refused him. In 1886 he appears to have offered himself as secretary to the philanthropic People's Palace in East London. He was disappointed not to be invited by Curzon to the meetings of the 'Souls' which began in 1889 – Margot Tennant (later Asquith, the model for *Dodo*), Balfour, Asquith, Maurice Baring and Meredith typified its membership, that blend of aristocracy and artistry of which Wilde dreamed. He himself was, however, simply an ambitious man-about-town waiting for a suitable 'break'.

He was never wealthy because his lifestyle dictated extravagance, and while sending money to his mother and equally improvident brother ('I enclose you a small piece of paper, for which reckless bankers may give you gold, as I don't want you to die': *L* 242) he could remonstrate with the income tax inspector: 'I wish your notices were not so agitating and did not hold out such dreadful threats. A penalty of fifty pounds sounds like a relic of mediaeval torture.'(*L* 242)

However, one event in this period had profound implications: during his wife's second pregnancy Wilde [51] met a seventeen-year-old Canadian boy due to go to Cambridge, Robert Ross (1869-1918), who devoted the rest of his life to Wilde. He later boasted that 'I was the first boy Oscar had' (i.e. sexually). This may be true, but it is plainly wrong to suppose that he was the first of Wilde's intimate boy-friends. For example, in the previous year Wilde had rediscovered Harry Marillier, now aged twenty, who had worked in his Salisbury Street lodgings five years earlier and was now at Peterhouse, Cambridge (he later wrote on Beardsley). Wilde wrote to him:

> There is an unknown land full of strange flowers and subtle perfumes, a land of which it is my joy of all joys to dream, a land where all things are perfect and poisonous. (*L* 185)

> You too have the love of things impossible. . . . I have never learned anything except from people younger than myself, and you are infinitely young.
> (*L* 181)

Marillier, Wilde noted, was 'psychological'.

Aimée Lowther (then about 15 years old) later told Lady Juliet Duff that Wilde had said to her: 'If you had been a boy you'd have wrecked my life.' (*L* 351) There were other infatuations almost coincidental with his marriage — all about twenty years old, notably Douglas Ainslie, Graham Robertson and later Lionel Johnson, Arthur Clifton and Charles Ricketts. In fact from 1886 Wilde regularly went to Oxford to see young men. In 1890 Johnson (1867-1902) wrote after his first meeting with Wilde: 'I am in love with him.' (*L* 245) This kind of reaction from an undergraduate to a man of letters prepared to flatter his youth and beauty was predictable. To a young actor to whom he sent a necktie Wilde wrote:

'I know you will look Greek and gracious.' (*L* 293)

[52]   The 'love that dare not speak its name' was already familiar to Wilde by 1887 when he wrote a sonnet (rare for him at that period), 'Un Amant de Nos Jours', beginning: 'The sin was mine; I did not understand' (*W* 806); he subsequently adapted it as 'The New Remorse' and gave it to Lord Alfred Douglas. Wilde did not set out to wreck young lives, and at base his antinomianism and alienation were caused by, and in turn encouraged, a deep-rooted cynicism. Like so many cynics, he was capable of natural and spontaneous affection, and his good humour usually masked his more private and personal preoccupations — as, for example, when at the unveiling of Gower's sculpture of Shakespeare at Stratford in 1888 he reported to Ross that the band 'played God Save the Queen in my honour' (*L* 225).

Wilde's meeting with Ross was not a turning-point in his life, as far as his interest in younger men was concerned, but it led to a permanent friendship of which there were very few in his life. His increased association with men of Ross's age, and in Ross's company, however, was a symptom of his restlessness, uneasiness and lack of self-confidence in his adopted society, which was demonstrated, both in his social behaviour and in his writing, by flippancy and frivolity.

Wilde the outsider typified the rebel. His rejection of reason was in fact equivalent to his antinomianism. Uranian poetry, vicious satire, farce, camp aestheticism, erotomania, even his own domestic parody of Victorian respectability, were symbols of his permanent inner unease. He had failed to integrate into society, into literature or into personal relationships, and the rest of his brief career was spent increasing the tensions between himself and the rest of the world. 'Sometimes I think that the artistic life is a long and lovely suicide, and am not sorry that it is so.' (*L* 185)

2
Hubris

The Critic as Artist

In 1889 Wilde was thirty-five years old. He was married with two small sons and a homosexual lover. Since his return from America and his marriage he had reached a stylistic plateau as a critic with steady if unremarkable success, but he needed the imaginative breakthrough which came with the publication of his essays and stories in the years 1889-91. In the six years leading up to his eclipse we see a rapid acceleration of his talents and emotional energies, as all the characteristics I have already identified became heightened and intensified in his sensation-seeking, resulting in a life which he later admitted was 'unworthy of an artist' (*L* 577). As far as his sexual activities were concerned, a police prosecution would probably have been inevitable at some stage in the next few years, while in his written work there developed a reckless mocking of the society which had only a limited tolerance for his type of vicious satire. 'The whole clinical picture of Oscar Wilde in the 'nineties is one of conspicuous madness.' (Brasol 229) As his iconoclasm became more psychopathic and more conspicuous, Wilde became more unstable, more vulnerable.

On a personal level, in these years, Wilde also extended his circle of acquaintances, using mainly the Café Royal as well as after-theatre restaurants, such as Willis's and Kettner's, and hotels like the Savoy. He

was in contact with a diverse number of London's
[54] artists; Henry Harland, John Lane and the circle of
The Yellow Book; W. E. Henley and the respectable
'anti-decadent' poets; Dowson, Lionel Johnson and
the Rhymers' Club; the acting fraternity, including
George Alexander, Herbert Beerbohm Tree and
Irving; younger satirists such as Max Beerbohm, E. F.
Benson, Ada Leverson ('the Sphinx') and Richard Le
Gallienne; artists like Rothenstein, Ricketts, Shannon,
Conder, Sickert and Beardsley; chief among the
critics, Arthur Symons, 'Vernon Lee' (i.e. Violet
Paget, whose example in aesthetic dialogue he closely
followed),[15] Henry James and Gosse; among his
own countrymen, Yeats, Moore and Shaw; among the
French, Louÿs, Bourget and Gide; among glittering
London society, Lady Desborough, Lady de Grey,
Lady Brooke (the Ranee of Sarawak), Princess Alice
of Monaco, even the Prince of Wales; politicians and
diplomatists (Haldane, Curzon, Balfour and Asquith);
salacious gossips and adventurers like Trelawny
Backhouse and Frank Harris — together with figures
from his earlier years, Ruskin, Pater, Whistler, Ellen
Terry, Lily Langtry, Boucicault, J. A. Symonds,
these are like the jewels offered by Herod to Salome,
'moons chained with rays of silver . . . fifty moons
caught in a golden net' (*W* 572).

Wilde had little contact with the Irish in London.
He and George Moore had a mutual antipathy; Wilde
disliked his 'vague, formless, obscene face' (*L* 778).
He did, however, meet Irish poets such as John
Todhunter and T. W. Rolleston, and he, his mother
and Willie joined the 'Irish Literary Society' (White
263). He was admired by Justin Huntly McCarthy
and caricatured by fellow-Dubliner Harry Furniss.
He also had some contact with political figures and
sympathisers such as Michael Davitt and Wilfrid
Scawen Blunt; he perceived Smith O'Brien and Parnell

as typically 'brilliant failures'. He had no intimates of equal intelligence or brilliance, and in fact no close friends — he was also generally on cool terms with Willie. Like his literary contacts, his personal relationships were tangential rather than direct.

His legendary table-talk dates from this time. It took three forms: firstly, quipping and bandying epigrams in cross-fire with other conversationalists like Frank Harris ('Of course Frank has dined in the best houses in London, *once*); secondly, in his parables and 'prose poems' such as 'The Doer of Good' although the more cynical and, perhaps, more revealing of these date from his last days in Paris); thirdly, his flights of fancy, which he himself described in a self-portrait in *Dorian Gray*:

> He played with the idea, and grew wistful; tossed it into the air and transformed it; let it escape and recaptured it; made it iridescent with fancy, and winged it with paradox. The praise of folly, as he went on, soared into a Philosophy. . . . It was an extraordinary improvisation. . . . He was brilliant, fantastic, irresponsible. He charmed his listeners out of themselves, and they followed his pipe laughing. (*W* 45)

During this time he grew away from his wife and family. Although he rehearsed some of his stories in the nursery and his younger son, Vyvyan, recalled his singing an Irish lullaby, *Tá mé i mo choladh, is ná dúisaigh mé*,[16] and he assiduously took the family on seaside holidays each year, yet his need to escape the inevitable domestic interruptions, and his increasing 'double life', meant that for long periods he was almost a guest in his own house. At first after his marriage Wilde tried to establish a salon like his mother's, while he remained the 'Apostle of Beauty' in the public eye. Constance was featured — or was it

satirised?– in the popular press as 'the Châtelaine of
[56] the House Beautiful', and as late as 1888 *The Lady's
Home Journal* (of Philadelphia) reported

> There is perhaps no house in London where more
> brilliant and delightful people congregate during
> the season, and where the talk is sure to be brilliant,
> as in the little salon presided over by Mrs Oscar
> Wilde. Poets, artists, sculptors, members of Par-
> liament, scientific men, actors and actresses, ladies
> of high title, men of lofty position, and the gilded
> youth of today gather together around Mrs Wilde's
> tea-table, attracted quite as much by the charm of
> the hostess as by the inimitable wit of her husband.

However, there was a gradual but general falling off
in attendances until the 'gilded youth' remained
almost alone, the most regular of them being Robert
Ross and Alfred Douglas, an Oxford undergraduate
introduced in 1891. Wilde grew increasingly bored
with Constance, who disapproved of his self-
aggrandisement and floridity. There is a great deal of
her in the brief portrait of Lady Henry Wotton in
The Picture of Dorian Gray, aware of her husband's
fascination with what Wilde perversely called 'strange
and troubling personalities walking in painted
pageants' (*L* 322). By 1891 his mother was caution-
ing him severely to pay more attention to his wife.
When he was in Paris she wrote to him: 'Constance
was here last evening. She is so nice always to me. I
am very fond of her. Do come home. She is very
lonely and mourns for you. Do not leave her all
alone.' (Hyde 133, 135)

Money was a constant anxiety. It was only with
the success of *Lady Windermere's Fan* in 1891, which
is said to have earned Wilde over £7,000, that he
began to have a large income, and even then it was
irregular and unpredictable, since it depended on the

whim of the public and the critics, and ultimately on Wilde's own ability to maintain and improve his standard of play-writing. In any case his natural extravagance absorbed most of his new wealth: he frequently travelled to France and entertained lavishly, giving valuable gifts such as gold cigarette cases and jewels to his pick-up boys, in addition to small cash payments. Avoiding creditors was a regular hazard: 'Writters come out at night and writ one, the roaring of creditors towards dawn is frightful, and solicitors are getting rabies and biting people.' (L 354) At the time of his imprisonment he owed Charles Wyndham £300 advanced on an unwritten play, and he had similar obligations elsewhere.

After his downfall Wilde accepted that he had been drifting uncontrollably: 'People whose desire is solely for self-realisation never know where they are going.' (L 488) This is especially true of his ambivalent private life after he seriously began pursuing boys, and particularly after the start of his affair with Alfred Douglas. For example, in August and September 1892 the Wildes were holidaying at Cromer, which he found 'excellent for writing and golf still better' (L 320); if Wilde told his wife that he was going golfing when in fact he was having homosexual assignations, it is strange that she was deceived when they were in the relatively enclosed world of a holiday house. Wilde's interest in boys was scarcely concealed, since in 1894 at Worthing he and Douglas, who was staying with them, openly brought back to the family luncheon the boys they had picked up on the beach. Perhaps Wilde did sometimes set off with a bag of clubs or even play a game in order to lay the foundation for a later subterfuge?[17]

The overriding characteristic which represents Wilde's public face in these years of hubris is his charm. Without his electric personality, his flamboyant appearance, increasingly 'fat and greasy' with a suggestion of sweaty palms and thighs and morbid caresses, would never have been accepted, even among his own coterie. In order to project his brilliant flights of talk, especially as they became more cynical, Wilde needed to act an attractive role. This is proved by the fact that he succeeded on occasions in winning the grudging but genuine admiration not only of the anti-decadent Henley (who was conducting a vendetta against him) and of his fellow-Irishman George Moore, who thoroughly disliked him, but also of the man who became his sworn enemy, the Marquess of Queensberry, whom he once flattered and entranced by discussing the Marquess's favourite subject, the non-existence of God.

W. B. Yeats (1865-1939) had a curious perception of Wilde, whom he met frequently in 1888 and 1889: 'a triumphant figure . . . a figure from another age, an audacious Italian fifteenth-century figure . . . his charm was acquired and systematised, a mask which he wore only when it pleased him' (*Autobiographies* 79).

By 1892 Wilde was obese, 'his elephantine body tightly stuffed into his clothes' (*IR* 199). Indulgence necessitated frequent purges, and in July of that year he went to Bad Homburg for the cure, his wife taking delight in writing: 'Oscar is at Homburg under a regime, getting up at 7.30, going to bed at 10.30, smoking hardly any cigarettes, and being massaged, and of course drinking waters.' (*L* 316) In the previous year after the opening of *Lady Windermere's Fan* he had been obliged to go to the South of France for his health. On another occasion he had gone to Paris 'to recruit' and had proceeded thence to Brighton because he was 'very ill' (*L* 289). In fact Wilde held the common Victorian faith in 'ozone' as a restorative, which as early as 1878 he had taken at Dieppe and Bournemouth.

*   *   *

Wilde's success in the theatre was spectacular and unexpected. If *Lady Windermere's Fan* had flopped, *A Woman of No Importance* would probably not have been brought on. Wilde would have remained a minor figure, reviewing, publishing essays — an elegant and committed, if slightly ludicrous, critic, a figure recognisable in Daudet's picture of the 'fat satisfied gossipy woman' (Morley 49) who had failed as a poet and a playwright but whose short stories and adaptations of his own talks were as much a delight to read as they had been to hear.

It is therefore easy to see why Wilde attributed so much importance to the role of the critic. A 'modern' version of the Pater philosophy would be a useful development. Wilde's principal critical writings are those contained in *Intentions*, published in volume form in 1891, and *The Soul of Man under Socialism* (1891 as an essay, 1895 as a volume). In 1891 he also published (in addition to *The Happy Prince*) *A House of Pomegranates* and *Lord Arthur Savile's Crime and other stories*.[18] The latter pieces were light social comedies, although displaying elements of his increasing cynicism; complementary, in his idiosyncratic way, to some of Gissing's and Machen's work. The so-called 'children's stories' began life in his sons' nursery but developed into prose poems too highly developed for younger minds to appreciate. His fertile imagination needed such outlets as an escape valve to prevent the mental breakdown so prevalent among those involved in creative work, whether it was poem-making, lecture-giving, book-reviewing, table-talking or, eventually, play-writing.[19]

In 'The Critic as Artist', the core of his critical theory and the key to his behaviour in this period, Wilde asserts that criticism is an art in itself and that the critic creates a work of art by appreciating one.

As a corollary, Wilde asserts that by use of his imagination the critic can express his personality through
his work: 'That is what the highest criticism really is,
the record of one's own soul.' (*W* 1027) Moreover,
Wilde claims that such a personal creation is an end in
itself – criticism for the sake of criticism – suggesting that the work of criticism might exist independent of the work of art to which it bears a tenuous
relationship. In this way a work of criticism can
enrich a work of art. To illustrate this Wilde makes
a commentary on Pater's famous criticism of the
'Mona Lisa':

> And so the picture becomes more wonderful to
> us than it really is, and reveals to us a secret of
> which, in truth, it knows nothing. (*W* 1029)

Wilde then develops beyond this the theory that,
because there is no direct connection between art and
morality, the critic has no moral obligations:

> The true critic . . . will never suffer himself to be
> limited to any settled custom of thought, or stereo-
> typed mode of looking at things. He will realise
> himself in many forms, and by a thousand different
> ways, and will ever be curious of new sensations
> and fresh points of view. Through constant change
> and through constant change alone, he will find his
> true unity. (*W* 1048)

Gradually Wilde reveals himself as an antinomian
and a narcissist. He disdains laws that restrict his personal freedom as a critic and becomes contemptuous
of 'the English mind' (see *W* 1056).

> Society which is the beginning and basis of morals
> . . . often forgives the criminal; it never forgives the
> dreamer. What is termed Sin is an essential element
> of progress. Without it the world would stagnate,
> or grow old, or become colourless. By its curiosity

Sin increases the experience of the race. Through its intensified assertion of individualism it saves [61] us from monotony of type. In its rejection of the current notions about morality, it is one with the higher ethics. (*W* 1023-4)

Finally Wilde announces that he hopes to attain a sinless existence which would consecrate the life of the artist; in the 'Hellenic' sense this means a state where *paederasteia* takes place on a spiritual level only, 'platonic' rather than erotic, as other Uranians such as Symonds had already insisted (see *Greek Poets*, first and second series):

> . . . the perfection of those to whom sin is impossible . . . because they can do everything they wish without hurt to the soul . . . able to transform acts or passions that with the common would be commonplace, or with the unconverted ignoble, or with the shameful vile. Is it dangerous? Yes, it is dangerous, – all ideas, as I told you, are so. (*W* 1058)

Forgiveness between Wilde and society was mutually impossible: 'I look forward to the time when aesthetics will take the place of ethics, when the sense of beauty will be the dominant law of life,' he wrote as a dreamer in 1890 when *Dorian Gray* was under attack. 'It will never be so, and so I look forward to it.' (*L* 265)

*   *   *

The Soul of Man under Socialism is an extremely confused document: the views expressed are ironical, satirical and insincere. For example, Wilde alleged that 'the people who do most harm are the people who try to do most good', that 'charity degrades and demoralises . . . creates a multitude of sins' (*W* 1079). In fact Wilde temporarily adopted socialism because it suited his egotism at that time: Socialism itself will be of value simply because it will lead to individualism.' (*W* 1080) In

anticipation of his selfish outpourings in 'De Profundis',
[62] Wilde says: 'He who would lead a Christlike life is he
who is perfectly and absolutely himself' — i.e. living
on his own terms. He cannot accept society's prior
authority as 'the beginning and basis of morals'. 'It is
the fact that Art is this intense form of Individualism
that makes the public try to exercise over it an
authority that is as immoral as it is ridiculous.'
(*W* 1090) He recognises that 'Individualism is a disturbing and disintegrating force' (*W* 1091) — he might
have been tempted to claim that the Greeks were the
first anarchists. He actually stated in 1893 that
whereas he had politically supported tyranny, he was
now an anarchist (Woodcock, *Anarchism* 285).

In declaring that 'the new Individualism is the new
Hellenism' (*W* 1104) Wilde was making explicit what
was implicit in the 1890s, the conflict of individualism
(as exemplified by himself, Alfred Douglas, Beardsley,
Henry James, Yeats, George Moore) with the stream
of collectivism which characterised Victorian success
and was typified by Henley, Newbolt, Watson, Kipling
and the popular (particularly the lady) novelists.

The Soul of Man under Socialism puzzled Wilde's
contemporaries; the *Spectator* called it 'unhealthy',
contemptuous of 'all law which restricts individualism' (Morley 76; Mason 52). *Intentions*, on the other
hand, seems to have deceived them, or at least to have
diverted their criticism. Yeats (*United Ireland*, 26
September 1891) called it 'some of the most subtle
literary criticism we are likely to see for many a long
day'. It is, of course, possible to read *Intentions* on
this level as a sincere development of Wilde's aestheticism, but we must remember that in 'The Critic as
Artist' Wilde wrote: 'What people call insincerity is
simply a method by which we can multiply our
personalities.' (*W* 1048) Wilde realised very early
that he was 'entirely free and at the same time entirely

dominated by law' (*L* 443), and in his writings he was exactly predicting his actions which were to test this hypothesis.

2
'Your Slim Gilt Soul'

At the outset of the decade which is so strongly associated with his name Wilde's novella, *The Picture of Dorian Gray*, appeared in the July 1890 issue of *Lippincott's Monthly Magazine*. Its tenor and critical reception were typical of the debate of the 1890s, which embraced genres as diverse as those of Ibsen and Wagner, Beardsley and Shaw, personalities as opposite as the cautious Henry James and the reckless Wilde; the call for novelty, artificiality and modernity, combined with a tendency to express things trivially — in cartoons, short stories, villanelles; a revival of interest in the illustration as a work of art; a meeting-point of aestheticism, symbolism, decadence, a vigorous anti-decadence, a dying imperialism in which the political events, like those on the stage, exhibited melodramatic qualities — the Jameson Raid, the Boxer Rebellion, Kitchener's initiative in the Sudan: a curiosity based on self-consciousness; revolutionary, evolutionary, degenerative and regenerative dynamics. The 1890s as a decade might be characterised as a mixed metaphor trying to embrace its own reputation. In this situation a man with interests and inclinations as disparate as those of Oscar Wilde was certain to find his level, both artistically and emotionally.

Wilde's career is important, symbolically, because the 1890s were concerned with the development of social life. Democratic, volatile, extrovert — social debate was concerned with everything; not Morris's socialism, but Shaw's; The decadence, defined by

Arthur Symons in 1893 as 'a moral and spiritual
[64] perversity . . . a new and beautiful and interesting
disease', was by 1899 in danger of having no more
substance than 'unsatisfied virtue masquerading as
uncomprehended vice'; as Holbrook Jackson said,
'The decadents were romantic in their antagonism to
current forms, but they were classic in their insistence
upon new.' (Jackson 57) *The Yellow Book* (first
issued in April 1894) demonstrated the fact that the
age was at a crossroads: together with Dowson, Le
Gallienne, Beerbohm, Benson, Beardsley, Symons,
Harland and Gosse (but not Wilde) were Saintsbury,
Watson, Arthur Waugh, Leighton, Garnett and
Nettleship; halfway stood James and Bennett. Yellow
was the colour of the Regency, alive, expansive;
mauve was the colour of the decadence. Writing in
1891 in *The Hobby Horse*, Lionel Johnson best
defined the age of decadence as one of 'afterthought,
of reflection . . . the virtue of meditation upon life,
its emotions and incidents; the vice of over-subtilty
and of affectation'.

It was therefore a healthy rather than a diseased
episode, in which, in addition to the decadents,
Kipling, Wells, Conrad and Belloc came to prominence.
It was also the age of the 'outsider': Wilde, Yeats,
Shaw, Moore, Whistler, Harris, Harland, James. Above
all the decade insisted on modernity and novelty —
the 'new paganism', the 'new woman', the 'new
hedonism', the 'new spirit', the 'new remorse'. Wilde
responded with his own brand of artificiality: 'The
first duty in life is to be as artificial as possible.'
(*W* 1205) His dandies were designed to be modern,
in the avant-garde. In his commonplace book he
noted: 'Not to conform is simply a synonym for
progress. Progress is simply the instinct for self
preservation.' (Shewan 108) His personal response,
besides his revolutionary attitude to drama, was the
Dorian Gray outlook:

I was so typical a child of my age that in my perversity and for that perversity's sake, I turned the [65]
good things of my life to evil, and the evil things
of my life to good. (*L* 469).

The main interest of *Dorian Gray*, the supreme
work of English decadent literature, for the biographer
is to see how much of himself Wilde put into it:

Basil Hallward is what I think I am. Lord Henry
what the world thinks of me. Dorian what I would
like to be — in other ages perhaps. . . . To the
world I seem by intention on my part a dilettante
and dandy, merely — it is not wise to show one's
heart to the world. . . . In so vulgar an age as this
we all need masks. (*L* 352-3)

Lord Henry's gospel says:

The aim of life is self-development. To realise
one's nature perfectly, that is what each of us is
here for. . . . Return to the Hellenic ideal. . . .
The only way to get rid of a temptation is to yield
to it. . . . Nothing can cure the soul but the senses,
just as nothing can cure the senses but the soul — A
new Hedonism — that is what our century wants. . . .
Youth! Youth! There is absolutely nothing in the
world but youth! (*W* 29-32)

Dorian Gray responds to this 'higher philosophy'
of *paederasteia* which leads to an intensification of
sensation-seeking, compelled by the idea that he
could control the degeneration of the soul-picture,
yet constantly returning to be confronted with the
mocking evidence of his downfall. This compulsion
may also give us a clue to Wilde's own feelings about
his increasingly bizarre appetites:

There are moments, psychologists tell us, when the
passion for sin, or for what the world calls sin, so

dominates a nature, that every fibre of the body, as every cell of the brain, seems to be instinct with fearful impulses. Men and women at such moments lose the freedom of their will. They move to their terrible end as automatons move. Choice is taken from them, and conscience is either killed, or if it lives at all, lives but to give rebellion its fascination, and disobedience its charm. (*W* 144) [This passage occurs in one of the chapters added by Wilde in 1891.]

In this novel Wilde reaches new heights of selfishness with strong narcissist inclinations of the most perverse kind ('He grew more and more enamoured of his own beauty, more and more interested in the corruption of his own soul': *W* 103), while his own prejudices against the society he was soon to ridicule in his plays make an appearance under the aegis of Lord Henry:

The one charm of marriage is that it makes a life of deception absolutely necessary to both parties.

(*W* 20)

... large overdressed dowagers and tedious Academicians (*W* 21)

... middle aged mediocrities so common in London clubs ... characteristic British faces that, once seen, are never remembered (*W* 135)

You forget that we are in the native land of the hypocrite. (*W* 118)

But Wilde's most characteristic display of inverted virtue was his angry — almost self-righteous — reaction to the newspaper criticism which greeted the appearance of *Dorian Gray* in *Lippincott's*. Wilde's reply (*L* 257-9) to the savage criticism of the *St James's Gazette* is central to his standpoint as an artist:

I am quite incapable of understanding how any work of art can be criticised from a moral stand- point. . . . I wrote this book entirely for my own pleasure.

The *Daily Telegraph* spoke of 'the mephitic odours of moral and spiritual putrefaction', while the *Scots Observer* probably got to the heart of the moral issue when it pointed out that while *Dorian Gray*

> is ingenious, interesting, full of cleverness, and plainly the work of a man of letters, it is false art — for its interest is medico-legal; it is false to human nature — for its hero is a devil; it is false to morality — *for it is not made sufficiently clear that the writer does not prefer a course of unnatural iniquity to a life of cleanliness, health and sanity*. . . . Mr Wilde has brains, and art, and style; but if he can write for none but outlawed noblemen and perverted telegraph-boys . . . (*L* 265, my emphasis)

This latter remark was a clear reference to the Cleveland Street scandal of the previous year in which Lord Arthur Somerset (son of the Duke of Beaufort), together with the Earl of Euston, had been implicated in a male-brothel scandal and had fled to Italy. Wilde, to his discomfort, had been brought out into the open as the author of a homosexual novel.

W. H. Smith & Son withdrew *Lippincott's* from their stalls. The publishers asked Wilde to discuss the matter with them and advised him to make Dorian live longer in misery and either commit suicide or repent and become a better character. Wilde did in fact tone down considerably some of the more blatantly homosexual passages; for example, he omitted the passages 'Rugged and straightforward as he was, there was something in his nature that was purely feminine in its tenderness' and 'I have worshipped you with far more romance of feeling than a man usually gives to a friend. Somehow I had never loved a woman'; 'the French school of *Decadents'* became 'the French school of *Symbolists'* (an interesting critical substitution), and 'a dangerous novel' became 'a wonderful novel'. But he retained a passage that was 'Uranian' in its evasiveness:

> The love that he bore him — for it was really love — had nothing in it that was not noble and intellectual. It was not that mere physical admiration of beauty that is born of the senses, and that dies when the senses tire. It was such love as Michael Angelo had known and Montaigne, and Winckelmann and Shakespeare himself. (*W* 97)[20]

Homosexuals in Britain were horrified by the publicity and the rumours about their activities which began to creep around. As J. A. Symonds (who found the book 'psychologically interesting') said, 'If the British public will stand this, they can stand anything', adding: 'I resent the unhealthy, scented, mystic, congested touch which a man of this sort has on moral problems.' (*CH* 78)

*   *   *

It is tempting for the biographer to say that at this point in Wilde's story the real Dorian Gray walked into his life. However, there had been several Oxford undergraduates in Wilde's life during the past five years, and although the aristocratic Lord Alfred Douglas (1870-1945), third son of the eighth Marquess of Queensberry (1844-1900, sponsor of the 'Queensberry rules' of boxing), was a flower of Oxford youth when at the age of twenty he met Wilde in 1891 ('the most beautiful young man alive and a fine poet', as Lionel Johnson described him at his introduction to Wilde: *Bosie* 44), he was not a Dorian Gray, lacking much of Gray's character and his sinister interests.

But Douglas, nicknamed 'Bosie' by his family, had a marked influence on Wilde, who seemed to be fascinated not only by his beauty but also by his social position and his ability as a poet, chiefly a sonneteer. The significant difference in their ages was sixteen years, while that between Mahaffy and Wilde, and that between Pater and Wilde, was fifteen. Max Beerbohm in 1893 thought Douglas 'obviously mad (like all his family I believe), but at the same time rather charming — a very pretty reflection of Oscar' (Cecil 74). His parents were divorced, and his father was certainly an eccentric figure, whose family hated him: when he died, shortly before Wilde in 1900, his sons went to Paris 'in deep mourning and the highest spirits' (*L* 816). There were numerous scandals associated with his name, the most notorious perhaps being the occasion on which he pursued the Prime Minister, Rosebery, to Homburg with a horsewhip, because of his (allegedly homosexual) association with Queensberry's eldest son, Viscount Drumlanrig.

The friendship was intermittent at first. During 1891 and the first part of 1892 they only met four times, according to Wilde. Their introduction had been carefully and deliberately arranged by Lionel Johnson. While it is clear that their extravagant and flamboyant behaviour did not begin until the following year, they already knew each other very well, and, since it was from the outset expected that they would be attracted, it is difficult to accept Wilde's assertion that the friendship only dated from May 1892 (see *L* 281). The internal evidence of the rewriting of *Dorian Gray* between the 1890 and 1891 editions shows that although many of the overtly homosexual passages were toned down, the arrival of Douglas on Wilde's consciousness had influenced

his conception of Dorian Gray — the revised version
does not consist 'mainly of elaboration' as Hart-Davis
suggests. For example, the phrase 'curious artistic
idolatry' creeps into Hallward's account of how
Dorian has come to dominate his art, replacing the
expression 'extraordinary romance' (*W* 24). The
prophetic passage in *Lippincott's*

> From the moment I met you, your personality
> had the most extraordinary influence over me.
> I quite admit that I adored you madly, extravag-
> antly, absurdly.

became in the 1891 version:

> You became to me the visible incarnation of that
> unseen ideal, whose memory haunts us artists,
> like an exquisite dream, I worshipped you. (*W* 93)

Other expressions of admiration are added: 'He is
absolutely necessary to me' (*W* 23); Dorian becomes
'Prince Charming! Prince of Life' (*W* 75); 'I only
know that I had seen perfection face to face and that
the world had become wonderful to my eyes — too
wonderful, perhaps, for in such mad worship there is
peril' (*W* 93); 'I grew more and more absorbed in
you . . . it had all been what art should be, unconscious, ideal and remote' (*W* 94); 'You were to me
such an ideal as I shall never meet again.' (*W* 122) If
there is any doubt that Wilde was influenced by
Douglas in the rewriting of *Dorian Gray* (and therefore that they met earlier than has been generally
supposed), it should be dispelled by Wilde's statement

> I knew you had feet of clay . . . When I wrote
> among my aphorisms that it was simply the feet
> of clay that made the gold of the image precious,
> it was of you that I was thinking. (*L* 464)

The aphorism referred to appears in one of the new

chapters of *Dorian Gray* (*W* 138).

For his part Douglas 'adored' Wilde 'because he [71] was brilliant and wonderful and fantastic and fascinating in his mind and in his conversation' (*Autobiography* 138). 'Even before I met Wilde', he recorded,

> I had persuaded myself that 'sins of the flesh' were not wrong [Douglas said they were 'contrary to Christian ethics but not to pagan ethics'] and my opinion was of course vastly strengthened and confirmed by his brilliantly reasoned defence of them, which may be said almost to have been the gospel of his life. (*Autobiography* 76)

The earliest surviving letter from Wilde referring to Douglas was ironically written to Ross in mid-1892 (*L* 314) and was calculated to annoy his former lover. It was written from the Royal Palace Hotel, Kensington, where he had taken rooms in order to work without interruption:

> My dearest Bobbie, Bosie has insisted on stopping here for sandwiches. He is quite like a narcissus — so white and gold. I will come either Wednesday or Thursday night to your rooms. Send me a line. Bosie is so tired: he lies like a hyacinth on the sofa, and I worship him.
> You dear boy. Ever yours   Oscar (*L* 314)

This is a strange letter, because, while it was certain to arouse jealousy in Ross, the description of the 'narcissus' and the 'hyacinth' is interrupted to suggest an assignation with his best boy-friend, confirming this in the last line — 'you dear boy'.

Wilde's romance with Douglas quickly became a love affair, rather than a sex affair. Their sexual tastes were similar, but they had little sexual interest in each other, preferring 'rough trade' and young boys. Wilde's surviving letters to Douglas form some

of the most poetic love-letters extant written from
[72] an older to a younger man — the typical Uranian
worship. On receiving a sonnet from Douglas he
wrote:

> My Own Boy . . . it is a marvel that those red rose-
> leaf lips of yours should have been made no less for
> music of song than for madness of kisses. Your
> slim gilt soul walks between passion and poetry. . . .
> Always with undying love, yours   Oscar (*L* 326)

After a lovers' tiff:

> Dearest of all Boys . . . you must not make scenes
> with me, they will kill me, they wreck the loveliness
> of life. I cannot see you, so Greek and gracious,
> distorted with passion. I cannot listen to your
> curved lips saying hideous things to me. You are
> the divine thing I want, the thing of grace and
> beauty; but I don't know how to do it. . . . Why
> are you not here, my dear, my wonderful boy?
> (*L* 336-7)

After a similar occasion (there were many):

> I am happy in the knowledge that we are friends
> again, and that our love has passed through the
> shadow and the night of estrangement and sorrow
> and come out rose-coloured as of old. Let us always
> be dear to each other, as indeed we have been
> always. (*L* 347-8)

Wilde invited Douglas to his family holiday house
at Worthing in terms of a desperate older man cling-
ing to the youthful vision, yet embarrassed by his
position of paterfamilias:

> She [the 'horrid Swiss governess'] is quite impos-
> sible. Also children at meals are tedious. Also, you,
> the gilt and graceful boy, would be bored. Don't
> come here. I will come to you. . . . *I can't live*

without you. You are so dear, so wonderful, I think
of you all day long, and miss your grace, your
boyish beauty, the bright sword-play of your wit,
the delicate fancy of your genius. . . . I have no
words for how I love you. (*L* 358)

You are the atmosphere of beauty through which I
see life; you are the incarnation of all lovely
things. . . . I think of you day and night . . . you
honey-haired boy. (*L* 363)

Even during his trials, when he must have reflected
on the sordid spectacle which his debauchery had
created, he had not begun to doubt Douglas's motives,
as he did later. On the opening day of his second trial
he wrote:

I love you, I love you, my heart is a rose which
your love has brought to bloom. . . . You have
been the supreme, the perfect love of my life; there
can be no other. . . .

O sweetest of all boys, most loved of all loves, my
soul clings to your soul, my life is your life, and in
all the worlds of pain and pleasure you are my
ideal of admiration and joy. (*L* 398)

As Wilde's infatuation with Douglas developed he
spent more time with him than with his family. The
rooms he had rented for work purposes — to finish
the plays urgently required by managers who had
paid substantial advances — became meeting-places
for the lovers. In addition, Wilde tried to reconcile
Douglas with his family, as he had previously with
Ross, bringing him to their seaside holidays. From
1892 to 1894 Wilde lived on a mad social roundabout,
punctuated by periods of intense work. On occasions
Douglas's interruptions were intolerable, and Wilde
resorted to extraordinary expedients, once even
leaving the country, 'giving my family some absurd

reason for my sudden departure' (*L* 433), but event-
[74] ually succumbing to Douglas's winsome entreaties
to rejoin him.

If Wilde as the author of 'De Profundis' (the letter
he wrote to Douglas from Reading prison) can be
believed, he spent a considerable part of 1894 reviewing his relationship with Douglas. He recalled 'thinking
what an impossible, terrible utterly wrong state my
life has got into . . . sadly and seriously trying to
make up my mind whether or not you really were
what you seemed to me to be' (*L* 433). Towards
the end of 1894, he said, he intended to use Sir
George Lewis as an intermediary with Queensberry in
formally severing his connections with Douglas, but
on the day in question Drumlanrig's death (thought
to be suicide) was announced. The Marquess's
opposition to their liaison was fierce; he was beginning the pursuit which led to public threats and
insults. Private gossip about their activities projected
their separate pederastic affairs onto their own
relationship, which was in fact becoming 'platonic',
while, with Wilde's arrogance and Douglas's youthful
indiscretion, it also grew more and more provocative.
There had been two clear precedents for the younger
sons of the peerage to be 'run out of town', and there
was an air of relief when it was announced that
Douglas (at his mother's and Wilde's urging) was
going abroad with a view to taking up a diplomatic
post in Egypt.

Lady Queensberry knew that Douglas had been
blackmailed at Oxford, and Wilde 'told her that your
life had been continually in the same manner
troubled' (*L* 434). If there was any doubt in his
mother's mind about his dependence on Wilde,
Douglas dispelled it:

Now let me ask you what you propose to give me
in exchange for this man, where am I to go for my

quickening? Who is going to 'feed my soul with honey of sweet bitter thoughts' [this was in fact [75] a phrase from a suitor's letter he had received from J. A. Symonds] . . . who is going to transport me out of this tedious world into a fairy land of fancy, conceit, paradox and beauty by the power of a golden speech? (*Bosie* 91)

Douglas's letters to his mother demonstrate an immature infatuation with a greater spirit. A young girl might have written similarly of the man she was determined to marry against parental opposition. He was not merely a spoilt, petulant child, angered if he could not have what he wanted; he was also tactless or thoughtless, speaking with a lack of consideration. For example, in one of his few surviving letters to Wilde (from Paris while Wilde was on bail between his first and second trials — an agonising period) he wrote:

Dieppe was too awful for anything; it is the most depressing place in the world, even Petits Chevaux was not to be had, as the Casino was closed. They are very nice here and I can stay as long as I like without paying my bill, which is a good thing as I am quite penniless. . . . Charlie [a mutual boyfriend] is with me and sends you his best love. (*L* 396)

For his part Wilde was writing:

Your love comes to me through my prison bars and comforts me. . . . Our love was always beautiful and noble. . . . I think that your love will watch over my life. (*L* 393-4)

It becomes easy to see how Wilde, during his two years' imprisonment, came to resent Douglas's extravagance and his apparently wilful disregard for anything except his own pleasure — an accusation, ultimately, of shallowness, the 'supreme vice' with which Wilde reproached him throughout 'De Profundis'.

Looking at the three years of their affair from the perspective of Reading prison, Wilde catalogues Douglas's personal faults: his idleness, his failure to appreciate Wilde as an artistic personality, his interruption of serious — and lucrative —work:

> I arrived at St James's Place every morning at 11.30. . . . At twelve o'clock you drove up, and stayed smoking cigarettes and chattering till 1.30, when I had to take you to luncheon at the Café Royal or the Berkeley. Luncheon with its *liqueurs* lasted usually till 3.30. For an hour you retired to White's. At tea-time you appeared again, and stayed till it was time to dress for dinner. You dined with me either at the Savoy or at Tite Street. We did not separate as a rule till after midnight, as supper at Willis's had to wind up the entrancing day. (*L* 426)

The chief problem was that both were immature personalities; each regarded the other as a toy, Douglas from an aristocratic standpoint, Wilde from an artistic. Each was capable of wounding the other. 'When you are not on your pedestal you are not interesting,' Douglas wrote to Wilde (*L* 439); later Wilde called him 'a gilded pillar of infamy' (*L* 693). 'Now and then', he accused him, 'it is a joy to have one's table red with wine and roses, but you outstripped all taste and temperance.' (*L* 428) As Shaw summed it up in 1931, 'You did one another far more harm socially than you could possibly have wrought by any extremity of sensual affection.' (Mary Hyde 3)

Wilde and Douglas soon found that they were hardly attracted to each other sexually, that in fact they shared a common interest in boys of the working class, a taste Wilde developed after about 1890. At his trial considerable evidence was adduced of solicited assignations from 1893 with valets, waiters, guardsmen, and newspaper-sellers.

With the publication of *Dorian Gray* and the mounting success of his plays, four of which were produced in four years, Wilde rose phenomenally in self-confidence, and his prodigious output was matched by an increasing exploration of the delights offered by both high society and the homosexual demi-monde. He became fascinated by the spectacle of vice and by his own involvement in it; gradually his wits grew less sharp, and he lost the self-control with which so far he had been modulating his taste of success. In his final year of freedom all caution, all restraint and all discrimination seem to have been abandoned: 'I ceased to be Lord over myself. I was no longer the Captain of my Soul, and did not know it.' (*L* 466) His associates, however, did realise this, and, as some kind of impending reaction to his personal crusade of decadence became obvious to all but himself, they began to stand off.

Wilde's taste for working boys was purely sexual, while with young actors and undergraduates he looked for more 'artistic' experiences. Douglas was for love: 'You are more to me than any one of these has any idea.' (*L* 363) Together (for example at Worthing) they picked up boys who became playthings to them. When Douglas returned to London Wilde sent him news of their favourites, 'Ernesto', Percy, 'Alphonso', Stephen and Henry:

Alphonso always alludes to you as 'the Lord', which however gives you, I think a Biblical Hebraic dignity that gracious Greek boys should *not* have. He also says, from time to time, 'Percy was the Lord's favourite', which makes me think of Percy as the infant Samuel — an inaccurate reminiscence, as Percy was Hellenic. (*L* 363)

Wilde was extremely sensitive to the implied sneers and rumours beginning to circulate about his private life, and he reacted strongly to quell any mutterings he heard (just as he had objected to criticism of *Dorian Gray*). In 1892 Rider Haggard wrote:

He is an amusing man though I wish he would drop his affectations! It seems from what he tells me the he feels the sneers and attacks on him. I thought they were the breath of his nostrils. Still I must say that if half what we hear is true, he has done a good deal to bring them on his own head.

(*Ross* 358)

When a love-letter to Douglas was stolen and a copy reached Herbert Beerbohm Tree, who was rehearsing *A Woman of No Importance*, Tree remarked to Wilde that the letter was open to mis-construction. Wilde replied that as a prose poem it might find its way into *The Golden Treasury*, brazenly arranging for Pierre Louÿs to make a French translation as a sonnet which Douglas published in his Uranian undergraduate magazine *The Spirit Lamp*. In the course of 1894 Wilde was approached several times by blackmailers with compromising letters such as that shown to Tree, but refused to be 'rented' as Douglas had been.

It was in *The Spirit Lamp* that Douglas published his sonnet 'Two Loves' which gave homosexuality its slogan of repression for the next two decades:

'What is thy name?' He said, 'My name is Love.' /
Then straight the first did turn himself to me / And [79]
cried, 'He lieth, for his name is Shame' . . . / Then
sighing said the other, 'Have thy will, / I am the
love that dare not speak its name.'

For a while Wilde tried to transpose into an artistic
key the sexual and social frisson which he got from
dining and sleeping with working boys:

People thought it dreadful of me to have entertained at dinner the evil things of life, and to have
found such pleasure in their company. But they,
from the point of view through which I, as an artist
in life, approached them, were delightfully suggest-
ive and stimulating. It was like feasting with
panthers. . . . They were to me the brightest of
gilded snakes. (L 492)

He thought of 'that tiger life' as presenting him
with a pageant of 'gracious things, in antique robes
and . . . gilded masks' (L 345). From Babbacombe,
Lady Mount-Temple's Pre-Raphaelite house which he
took in 1893, he wrote to a young actor: 'I want you
down here; it is a lovely place, and you need rest
and quiet, and I need you too. . . . You are an
artist. . . . You are my ideal friend. (L 323-4)
Constance having shown some independence by
going alone on holiday to Italy, Wilde was left at
Babbacombe in charge of Cyril and Vyvyan. He
invited Douglas and his tutor to stay. The latter
reported to Johnson:

Our life is lazy and luxurious; our moral principles
are lax. We argue for hours in favour of different
interpretations of Platonism. Oscar implores me,
with outspread arms and tears in his eyes, to let
my soul alone and cultivate my body for six weeks.
Bosie is beautiful and fascinating, but quite

wicked. . . . I think [Wilde] perfectly delightful,
[80]   with the firmest conviction that his morals are
detestable. (*L* 867-8)

At this time Max Beerbohm wrote to a mutual
homosexual friend some extremely revealing gossip
which illuminates like a lexicon most of the characteristics of the homosexual world of the day:

A schoolboy with wonderful eyes, Bosie, Bobbie
[i.e. Ross], a furious father, George Lewis, a head-
master (who is now blackmailing Bobbie). . . .
Calais, Dover, Oscar Browning, Oscar, Dover, Calais,
intercepted letters, private detectives, Calais, Dover,
and returned cigarette cases were some of the
ingredients in the dreadful episode. . . . The schoolboy the same as him of whom I told you that he
had been stolen from Bobbie by Bosie and kept
at the Albemarle Hotel. (Beerbohm, *Letters* 84)

The Albemarle Hotel was a customary rendezvous
for such *liaisons dangereuses*, and it is interesting
that one of the only two occasions on which it was
alleged that Wilde was in bed with a boy was at this
particular time at this particular place, an accusation
which he said should fairly have been levelled not at
him but at Douglas, who actually had the boy – a
claim which this letter seems to support. Cigarette
cases were Wilde's regular parting gift to his pick-ups;
the Dover/Calais crossing was used by many homosexuals for one of three reasons – to take a boy-
friend to France for a 'dirty weekend', to go over to
'gay Paris' or Dieppe to cruise unrecognised, or as
an escape valve if activities at home became too hot.
Visits to France were less detectable. In late 1891
Wilde met and befriended André Gide, and it seems
that he strongly influenced the twenty-two-year-old
Frenchman towards homosexuality at the time. One
of Gide's friends noticed an infatuation with Wilde

(Hyde 129), who, for his part, in 1897 said: 'I love André personally very deeply.' (*L* 590)[21] An introduction to Proust, also in 1891, proved unsuccessful. During this visit the gossip paper *Echo de Paris* announced Wilde as 'one of the most interesting personalities in contemporary English literature' and described his visit as 'le "great event"' of Parisian literary salons.

It was inevitable that private scandals would eventually become public knowledge. There had been several in the past ten years, and one of the first convictions under the 1885 act was obtained in 1893 when an Irish MP, Edward de Cobain, a former Grand Master of the Grand Orange Lodge of Belfast, was convicted of acts of gross indecency. Others like the Somerset brothers and the transvestite Marquess of Anglesey were luckier, escaping or being sent abroad.

In 1894 Beerbohm, not yet famous for his caricatures, but espousing the dandyish form of belles-lettres, wrote an essay proposed for *The Yellow Book* (which cautiously rejected it): 'A Peep into the Past' satirised Wilde as an old man who

> is something of a martinet about punctuality in his household, and perhaps this accounts for the constant succession of page-boys which so startles the neighbourhood. . . . As I was ushered into the little study I fancied that I heard the quickly receding frou-frou of tweed twousers, but my host I found reclining hale and hearty, though a little dishevelled, upon a sofa. (*Peep into the Past* 11-14)

At Wilde's trial it was in fact alleged that he had had sexual relations with boys at his home in Tite Street, although it is difficult to credit this. What is certain, however, is that Wilde's activities spurred him on to further reaches of self-confidence and, ultimately, self-deception. As Lionel Johnson said, he acquired his sense of triumph and power, at every dinner-table he dominated, from the knowledge that he was guilty of that sin which, more than any other possible to man, would turn all these people against him if they but knew. (Yeats, *Autobiographies* 285)

What 'that sin' actually was, is, however, difficult to define: it was certainly not sodomy (i.e. *pedicatio*, or anal penetration) which held little interest for Wilde, his favourite activities being *fellatio*, mutual masturbation and inter-crural orgasm; nor could he be accused of the 'corruption of youth' as far as sexual offences were concerned, although his intellectual influence was very marked. The 'sin' that Johnson diagnosed resulted from the combination of an Uranian or pederastic mentality with an egotistic, antinomian intellect, and its effect was to throw hypocrisy and inconsistency into high relief while advocating a form of moral anarchy (in Victorian terms) masked as artistic licence.

This influence, under a cloak of bizarre frivolity, pervaded the artistic circles in which Wilde moved: his own tables at the Café Royal or Willis's, the meetings of the Rhymers' Club, even the editorial rooms of *The Yellow Book*. The most obvious example of his influence was on the personality of Richard Le Gallienne (1866-1947), whose life became an aesthetic adventure after his early exposure to Wilde's gospel. Others who came close were Max Beerbohm (1872-1956), Reginald Turner (1869-1938) and E. F. Benson (1867-1940, son of the Archbishop of Canterbury), whose families tried to prevent their association with Wilde.

The net began to close around Wilde's associates as police surveillance increased after the Cleveland Street scandal. On 12 August 1894 Alfred Taylor, a procurer known and patronised by Wilde, was arrested during a police raid on a homosexual club. It was alleged that he had gone through a form of marriage ceremony with Charles Mason, to whom Wilde wrote about the arrest: 'It is a dreadful piece of bad luck. . . . Let me know how you yourself are going on in your married life [*sic*] . . . . When I come back to town do come and dine. What fun our dinners were in the old days. I hope marriage has not made you too serious? It has never had that effect on me.' (*L* 363-4) The colleagues of one boy, Edward Shelley, to whom he had made advances, nicknamed him 'Mrs Wilde', to Shelley's embarrassment.)

Towards the end of 1894 Wilde's social position was obviously under threat. Attending a performance at the Haymarket he recorded:

> The bows and salutations of the lower orders who thronged the stalls were so cold that I felt it my duty to sit in the Royal Box with [the Queen's Private Solicitor, the Master of Buckhounds and the Home Secretary, Asquith] : this exasperated the wretches. How strange to live in a land where the worship of beauty and the passion of love are considered infamous. (*L* 377)

The height of Wilde's double game was perhaps the first night of *An Ideal Husband* (3 January 1895), which was attended by the Prince of Wales and by a large number of young men whom Wilde had persuaded to wear the green carnation, the badge of the Parisian homosexual.

From prison Wilde wrote that

> I used to rely on my personality: now I know that my personality really rested on the fiction of *position*. Having lost position, I find my personality of no avail. (*L* 791)

Apart from his success as a playwright, most of
[84] Wilde's 'position' can be attributed to the purchasing
power of his purse for the many hangers-on attracted
by his personal aura. He encouraged the adulation
lacking in his own home, and he developed a false
sense of security, believing himself equal to the aristo-
crats of the Victorian Empire who became the
targets of his satire. In fact Wilde became disenchanted
with the *embourgeoisement* of all levels of society,
and this accentuated his acidity. Society, for its part,
treated him as an entertainer, a plaything. The fact,
for example, that it was his 'spellbinding' dinner
conversation which persuaded George Alexander to
commission a society comedy indicates that it was
Wilde's flippancy, the sharpness of his Irish repartee,
and the frivolity of his mannerisms which made him
noticed, accepted and demanded in London salons
and weekend country houses. It is therefore ironic
that he should have used these comedies to throw
back into society's face the paradoxes of its
mannerisms, conventions and scandals, sending his
audiences home with their morals round their necks
like a string of sausages. Moreover, it was only certain
sections of Victorian society – the aristocracy and
haute bourgeoisie – which permitted themselves to
be so dazzled. Gentlemen's clubs and middle-class
drawing-rooms, and the newspapers read there,
resented his effrontery and his implied moral character.

Wilde began to be caricatured not only on the
familiar aesthetic grounds but also more personally.
The Green Carnation clearly exposed Wilde's mannerisms and inclinations in its portrait of 'Esmé Amarinth'
and his companion 'Lord Reginald Hastings'. Meanwhile Beardsley caricatured Wilde as a hermaphrodite,
it is said in revenge for Wilde's assertion that, in
addition to having invented the decade and the green
carnation, he had invented Aubrey Beardsley.

The German criminologist Max Nordau examined Wilde under the heading 'Ego-Mania' in *Degeneration* (1895), identifying his 'hysterical craving to be noticed, to occupy the attention of the world with himself, to get talked about' (p. 317). This was not an indication of independence of character but 'a purely antisocialistic, ego-maniacal recklessness and hysterical longing to make a sensation . . . a malevolent mania for contradiction' (p. 319). Analysing Wilde's essays (mainly *Intentions*), Nordau concluded that 'Wilde apparently admires immorality, sin and crime' (p. 320), and in considering antinomianism in art he asserts: 'The artist who complacently represents what is reprehensible, vicious, criminal, approves of it, perhaps glorifies it, differs not in kind, but only in degree, from the criminal who actively commits it.' (p. 326)

The police were not, however, the initial cause of Wilde's uncovering, which was due to the activities of a 'furious father', aided by the recklessness of both Douglas and Wilde, who with triple entendre wrote: 'I often betray myself with a kiss.' (*L* 373) The first real sign of trouble for Douglas and Wilde came in the summer of 1894 when Wilde wrote to his lover:

> Your father is on the rampage again — been to the Café Royal to enquire for us, with threats etc. I think now it would have been better for me to have had him bound over to keep the peace, but what a scandal! Still, it is intolerable to be dogged by a maniac. (*L* 360)

Although Queensberry was generally regarded as a blackguard and an unstable personality, he was openly swearing vengeance on Wilde for having seduced his son. Neither Wilde nor Douglas tried to conceal their affair. Douglas carried, for self-defence, a pistol which by way of demonstration he once let

off in a restaurant. In May 1894 Wilde had consulted
his solicitor about a libellous letter he had received
from Queensberry. He was dissuaded from instituting
proceedings, although the solicitor demanded an
apology, which Queensberry refused to give. Up to
this point Sir George Lewis had acted for Queensberry,
but he now refused to continue.

But even without 'the screaming scarlet Marquess',
as Wilde called him, there would probably have been
a scandal, for in 1895 Constance was considering a
divorce or a judicial separation in order to remove the
children, then aged ten and nine, from their father's
custody. Such an action would have constituted a
public exposé. It is in any case clear that at the time
the crisis broke, Wilde and his wife had been 'living
apart' — Constance scarcely expected to see him at
Tite Street. The scandal would probably have resulted
in Wilde going to live abroad, making cautious and
respectable visits to London at auspicious moments.
Whether he would have continued to write his
successful plays is debatable: self-effacement, to
which he was ill-suited, was the normal course for
exiled Uranians. He would simply have continued as
'the spendthrift of my own genius' (*L* 466).

4
'He Plays with Everything'

George Alexander produced *Lady Windermere's
Fan* at the St James's Theatre, London, on 20
February 1892. Overnight it made Wilde's reputation
as a dramatist. A. B. Walkley, an influential critic,
said in the *Speaker*:

> If we have had more sparkling dialogue on the
> stage in the present generation, I have not heard
> it. . . . The man or woman who does not chuckle
> with delight at the good things which abound . . .

should consult a physician at once, delay would be dangerous. [87]

Wilde had been impressed by Alexander's straight offer of £1,000 for the play, but he rejected it, realising what it meant: 'As I have such complete faith in your judgement, I will not take it — I will take a good percentage instead.' (*Ross* 152) Previously he had grandly demanded £200 for a play, since 'I fear I could not give up my paying work for speculative. I have to work for certainties.' (*L* 276)

Clement Scott, for the *Illustrated London News*, having suggested that Wilde 'is a cynic of deeper significance than we take him to be', analysed the author's 'intentions' in writing the play, putting these words into Wilde's mouth:

Society will not say one word except that it is all very amusing. Amusing they will consider it, but unnatural — never. *It is society that is at fault, not I.* I paint what I see; I am not a sentimentalist, but a cynic. The best test of the justice of my picture is found in the fact that *society does not reprimand it.* . . . They will laugh at what is clever. They love 'smart things'. They have canonised the word 'smart' . . . 'To be intelligible is to be found out.' I have never since I left Oxford . . . been wholly intelligible. And *I have never been found out.* (*CH* 124-6, my emphasis)

Wilde was in fact in the forefront of the 'new drama' movement, inspired by Ibsen, in the unlikely company of Pinero and Henry Arthur Jones, in that he was both modern and popular. This popularity grieved Henry James, who thought all Wilde's plays 'infantile', 'puerile' (see Edel); coming away from *An Ideal Husband* (while his own *Guy Domville* was playing to near-empty houses), he complained: 'The thing seemed to me to be so helpless, so crude, so

bad, so clumsy, feeble and vulgar. How *can* my piece
[88] do anything with a public with whom *that* is a
success?' (James, *Letters* I 233)

Wilde's first first-night speech is evidence of his
personal conceit and contempt:

> Ladies and Gentlemen, I have enjoyed this evening
> *immensely*. The actors have given us a *charming*
> rendering of a *delightful* play, and your apprec-
> iation has been most intelligent. I congratulate you
> on the *great* success of your performance, which
> persuades me that you think *almost* as highly of
> the play as I do myself. (Hyde 137)

This curtain speech was regarded as outrageous by
most present, mainly because Wilde came on stage
with a lighted cigarette, but it did not diminish the
success of the play, which ran for 156 nights.

With his next play, *A Woman of No Importance*,
Wilde tried to continue his personal crusade with an
outburst against Puritanism which his producer, Tree,
successfully insisted should be cut:

> The real enemy of modern life, of everything that
> makes life lovely and joyous and coloured for us,
> is Puritanism and the Puritan spirit. *There* is the
> danger that lies ahead for the age, and most of all
> in England. The wildest profligate who spills his
> life in folly, has a better, saner, finer philosophy
> in life than the Puritan has. (Hyde 155)

Wilde was a difficult author to produce, because he
insisted on attending and interrupting rehearsals.
Asked if he had produced the play with assistance of
Wilde, Tree replied: 'With the interference of Wilde.'
(Hyde 155) Again he was offensive to his audience,
which on the first night, 19 April 1893, at the Theatre
Royal, Haymarket, included Balfour and Joseph
Chamberlain. He announced: 'Ladies and gentlemen,

I regret to inform you that Mr Oscar Wilde is not in the house', before going on stage to take his curtain- call, to be greeted with hoots and hisses, besides vigorous applause.

> You are now the great sensation of London and I am very proud of you [his mother wrote]. You have made your name and . . . now take a distinguished place in the circle of intellects. . . . Take care of yourself and of your health and keep clear of suppers and late hours and champagne. Your health and calm of mind is most important.
> (Hyde 159)

Wilde's success, however, did depend on socialising, which inevitably undermined his health and imperilled his mental equilibrium. His talent fed on his genius, which in this case was his table-talk. In fact Ross acted for a time as his amanuensis, taking down quips which provided the copy for *The Importance of Being Earnest* and perhaps the earlier plays. As Wilde said through Lord Illingworth, 'To get into the best society nowadays, one has to feed people, amuse people or shock people' (*W* 460); Illingworth also said: 'A man who could dominate a London dinner-table can dominate the world' (*W* 459) – an idea Wilde had probably heard from Mahaffy. On the other hand, he also knew that a 'professional story-teller' can be 'a great bore at a dinner-table' (*R* 242).

Not only was Wilde capable of general, imitable witticisms (e.g. 'Surely Providence can resist temptation by this time' or 'Work is the curse of the drinking classes' or 'He hasn't a single redeeming vice'), but he also developed his own contribution to the field of creative humour. For example, Wilde's view of Judas Iscariot as a *nouveau riche*, or his assertion that he should not pay rates on the house where he slept because he slept so badly, establish a new logical relationship of one idea with another.

Thus a character in *The Importance of Being Earnest* finds clerical celibacy the reason why the Primitive Church has not survived; another must be in London in order to miss an appointment *because* the appointment is in London. Wilde greets another guest at a reception with the words 'I'm so glad you have come, there are so many things I want not to say to you'; and when the publisher Osgood, whose books were announced as being published simultaneously in London and New York, died, Wilde said: 'I suppose they will bury him simultaneously in London and New York.' In terms of drama, Wilde not only put such logical improbabilities in the mouths of his characters, as, for example, in the first version of *The Importance of Being Earnest* where Lady Bracknell refers to Ernest as 'a person . . . the fact of whose very birth seems extremely problematic', but he also used the technique of bisociation to create a counterpoint between natural comedy and the absurdity of his situations, by which he maintained a most brilliant form of satire within the boundaries of farce.

Before the production of *A Woman of No Importance* Max Beerbohm wrote to his close friend Reggie Turner:

> I am sorry to say that Oscar drinks more than he ought. . . . He has deteriorated very much in appearance, his cheeks being quite a dark purple and fat to a fault. I think he will die of apoplexy. (Hyde 156)

He was also, as usual, financially embarrassed. While he was writing *An Ideal Husband* in mid-1894 he told George Alexander: 'I am so pressed for money that I don't know what to do.' (*L* 359) And to Douglas he complained: 'It is really intolerable the want of money. I have not got a penny. I can't stand it any longer.' Large income from successful plays only relieved the mounting debts. Royalties of £300 from Alexander were swallowed up by writs for £400, 'rumours of prosperity having reached the commercial classes.... I am sorry my life is so marred and maimed by extravagance. But I cannot live otherwise.' (L 383-4)

Wilde wrote not only society comedies or tragi-comedies at this time. In 1892 he also wrote *Salome*, his one successful biblical drama, which Sarah Bernhardt began to rehearse. The Lord Chamberlain, the official censor of plays, refused a licence on the grounds that no biblical character might be portrayed on stage. The rehearsals closed, and Wilde announced his intention to live in France:

I will not consent to call myself a citizen of a coun-try that shows such narrowness in its artistic judge-ment. I am not English — I am Irish — which is quite another thing. (Mason 373)

The *Times* described *Salome* on publication as 'an arrangement in blood and ferocity, morbid, bizarre, repulsive, and very offensive in its adaptation of scriptural phraseology to situations the reverse of sacred' (*CH* 133). Wilde had originally written *Salome* in French, with corrections by Adolphe Retté, Pierre Louÿs and Stuart Merrill ('les erreurs manifestes'). According to Merrill, Wilde wrote French 'in a fan-tastic way which, while it was stylish in conversation, would in the theatre have produced a deplorable impression' (L 305). Marcel Schwob, to whom Wilde dedicated *The Sphinx* and who died in 1905 of a syphilitic tumour in the rectum, corrected the proofs. It was translated by Douglas, but Wilde did not like the English version and revised it before publication.[22]

A further aspect of Wilde's play-writing at this stage is the hardly realised fact that he was still pursuing the idea of verse drama which had begun with *The Duchess of Padua*. In fact, rather than relinquishing 'serious' drama for comedy, Wilde was quite deliberately alternating his dramatic interests. Interspersing *Lady Windermere's Fan* and *A Woman of No Importance* with *Salome*, he next attempted a second 'biblical' drama, *La Sainte Courtisane* or 'The Woman Covered with Jewels' (*W* 701-5), similar to the Salome theme. At the same time he began a blank-verse play, *A Florentine Tragedy* (*W* 689-700). He put this aside in order to work on the more lucrative prospect of *An Ideal Husband*, taking it up and abandoning it once more when the cistern had filled for *The Importance of Being Earnest*.

Two further projects were begun before imprisonment. After writing most of *The Importance of Being Earnest* in 1894 Wilde jotted down the scenario of another 'good woman' play, which he intended to call *Constance*, subsequently staged as *Mr and Mrs Daventry*; this suggests that rather than continue with the brilliant farce, he might have returned to more conventional and melodramatic tragi-comedies. Finally, the sketch exists, also dating from 1894, of *The Cardinal of Avignon*, another medieval drama (printed in Mason 183-5), and another 'good woman' subject, *A Woman's Tragedy* (Dulau, item 1).

An indication of how Wilde's dramatic style might have developed is given in his description of the scenario of *Mr and Mrs Daventry*:

> *I want the sheer passion of love to dominate everything*. No morbid self-sacrifice. No renunciation. A sheer flame of love between a man and a woman. That is what the play is to rise to — from the social chatter of Act I, through the theatrical effectiveness of Act II, up to the psychology with its great *dénouement* in Act III, till love dominates Act IV

and accepts the death of the husband as in a way its proper right, leaving love its tragedy, and so making it a still greater passion. (*L* 361-2)

A further aspect of his views on the stage (also revealing something of his attitude to life) dates from a remark reported by the *Daily Telegraph* (12 February 1892) that the stage is only a frame furnished with a set of puppets, i.e. the symbolist marionettes taken up by Yeats and Appia. Wilde retaliated that he had actually referred to the stage as 'peopled with either living actors or moving puppets', arguing:

There are many advantages in puppets. They never argue. They have no crude views about art. They have no private lives. They recognise the presiding intellect of the dramatist and have no personalities at all (*L* 311)

Although there was therefore considerable alternation in Wilde's mind between at least two main forms of dramatic expression, in the years from 1891 to 1894 there is no doubt that his major achievement was the production of two plays which, with hindsight, mark the apogee of his short career: *An Ideal Husband* and *The Importance of Being Earnest*.

Wilde's four society dramas have two elements in common: firstly they all feature a 'woman with a past' (including Miss Prism in *The Importance of Being Earnest*); secondly, they all mark the arrival of the dandy on the melodramatic scene. In the first, Wilde was in the same company as Shaw's *Mrs Warren's Profession* and Pinero's *The Second Mrs Tanqueray* (both, like *A Woman of No Importance*, produced in 1893); in the second, he made a unique contribution to the development of English drama.

Although critics of his earlier plays had asked for

less epigrams, *An Ideal Husband* glitters even more
brilliantly than its predecessors. As an example of a
straight comedy with little philosophising or moral-
ising, a 'camp' society satire, it is unrivalled, even by
The Importance of Being Earnest. Even his stage
directions are 'camp' — the height of perversity —
equalling some of Yeats's in their impossibility:

> They are types of exquisity fragility. Their affect-
> ation of manner has a delicate charm. Watteau
> would have loved to paint them. (*W* 482)

> She looks rather like an orchid, and makes great
> demands on one's curiosity. . . . A work of art,
> on the whole, but showing the influence of too
> many schools. (*W* 484)

Wilde's jeers at 'Society' are more pronounced: 'It is
entirely composed now of beautiful idiots and brilliant
lunatics.' (*W* 484)

In a series of clever paradoxes he succeeds in turning accepted morality on its head and showing that
the traitorous past conduct of Sir Robert Chiltern
was in fact a virtuous act, for which the establishment
rewards him:

> Do you really think that it is weakness that yields
> to temptation? I tell you that there are terrible
> temptations that it requires strength, strength and
> courage, to yield to. To stake all one's life on a
> single moment, to risk everything on one throw,
> whether the stake be power or pleasure, I care not —
> there is no weakness in that. There is a horrible,
> a terrible courage. I had that courage. . . . I felt
> I had fought the century with its own weapons and
> won. (*W* 506)

As a foil to Chiltern and the wicked Mrs Cheveley,
Wilde presents the arch-dandy, Lord Goring. In *A*

Woman of No Importance he had asserted: 'The future belongs to the dandy' (*W* 459), and Goring himself 'stands in immediate relation to modern life, makes it indeed, and so masters it'. 'The only possible society', declares Lord Goring, 'is oneself. . . . To love oneself is the beginning of a lifelong romance.' (*W* 522)

Shaw, in a tongue-in-cheek article in the *Saturday Review*, saw what Wilde was doing:

> He plays with everything, with wit, with philosophy, with drama, with actors and audience, with the whole theatre. Such a feat scandalises the Englishman . . . the total result being the Englishman utterly unconscious of his real self, Mr Wilde keenly observant of it and playing on the self-consciousness with irresistible humour, and finally, of course, the Englishman annoyed with himself for being amused at his own expense. He is shocked, too, at the danger to the foundations of society when seriousness is publicly laughed at (*CH* 176-8)[23]

With *The Importance of Being Earnest* Wilde emerged as a blatant iconoclast; his satire is not just unpleasant, but also sinister and highly destructive. The play is the first decadent comedy in the English language.

It is surprising that Arthur Symons failed to appreciate this aspect of *The Importance of Being Earnest*, calling it 'a sort of sublime farce, meaningless and delightful'. Shaw, while he thought it extremely funny, said it was 'essentially hateful, his first really heartless play'. Walkley called it 'sheer nonsense'. Archer said it 'imitates nothing, represents nothing, means nothing, is nothing'. However, Shaw was very close to the truth when he called it hateful and heartless. It was a premeditated farce, in the sense that the incidents are bizarre and the situations comic, but its characters are far more sinister symbols of decadence than those of Wilde's earlier plays.[24] A man whose whole life is given up to pleasure, and who accuses the lower orders of a lack of exemplary moral responsibility, has gone beyond Villiers de L'Isle Adam's Axel or his own creator's Goring. Lady Bracknell, Gwendolen Fairfax, Cecily Cardew, Algernon and Jack are not just vicious caricatures but acid portraits of unashamed decadence. The sentiments expressed are profoundly disturbing, not just shocking, many of them being based on the deteriorating conditions of Wilde's private life:

Divorces are made in heaven. (W 323)

The truth isn't the sort of thing one tells to a nice, sweet, refined girl. (W 336)

Algernon: In married life three is company and two none.

Jack: That ... is the theory that the corrupt French Drama has been propagating for the last fifty years.

Algernon: Yes, and that the happy English home has proved in half the time. (W 327)

Once a man begins to neglect his domestic duties he becomes painfully effeminate, does he not? (W 362)

Wilde firmly plants the standard of cynicism:

Algernon: I hope tomorrow will be a fine day, Lane.

Lane: It never is, sir.

Algernon: Lane, you're a perfect pessimist.

Lane: I do my best to give satisfaction, sir. (W 338-9)

Perhaps the most telling declaration of war was Wilde's characterisation of Lady Bracknell; not only scheming, grasping, admiring of 'the purple of commerce', as absurd as Herod (I forbid him to raise the

the dead': *W* 565), she is no less unscrupulous and decadent in her outlook than Algernon and Ernest, and much less playful. Putting forward the perverted view that 'a girl with a simple unspoiled nature like Gwendolen could hardly be expected to reside in the country',[25] Lady Bracknell, following *Dodo*, becomes the second female dandy, and the first on the English stage.

Once again Wilde made himself a nuisance at rehearsals, objecting to the play's reduction from four acts to three, which necessitated cutting a scene which 'cost me terrible exhausting labour and heart-rending nerve-wracking strain. . . . It must have taken fully five minutes to write.' (Hyde 174) He went off with Douglas to Algiers, where they joined forces on a boy-hunt with André Gide, who told his mother: 'He has grown old and ugly, but as always an extra-ordinary talker.' Wilde left Douglas with Gide, returning just in time for the opening on 14 February 1895 — 'the last first night', the gossip columnist Ada Leverson called it. Despite attempts by Queensberry to disturb the première, it was an unparalleled triumph. 'In my fifty-three years of acting', Allan Aynsworth recalled, 'I never remember a greater triumph. . . . The audience rose in their seats and cheered again and again.' (Hyde 196)

Wilde, by being unintelligible with his 'nonsense', had once more escaped discovery by the critics. But four days later the infuriated Queensberry left a card at the Albemarle Club addressed 'For Oscar Wilde, posing sodomite [*sic*]'.[26] This action brought matters to a head as Queensberry intended, pre-cipitating what Henry James called 'an earthquake — social, human, sexual' (Edel II 201).

3
Nemesis

1
Dogged by a Maniac

Wilde now decided to act, convinced that he was defending Douglas from his father and removing any further threats to himself. But although he believed that 'I thought but to defend him from his father. I thought of nothing else' (*L* 390), Wilde's prosecution of Queensberry for criminal libel attempted much more, principally to defend his love of Douglas rather than Douglas himself. His actions seem to be hall-marked by ambivalence and indecision, swayed in one direction by Douglas, who was determined to see his father in the dock, in another by friends who counselled silence or flight.[27] Sir George Lewis afterwards said that if Wilde had gone to him with Queensberry's card he would simply have torn it up. But Wilde had diminished his credit with Lewis by interceding with him more than once on behalf of Douglas and others to avert blackmailing scandals. 'I began to lose his esteem and friendship,' Wilde later recalled, '. . . When I was deprived of his advice and help and regard I was deprived of the one great safeguard of my life.' (*L* 440)

After imprisonment he could reflect on how easily he had fallen into the trap:

His father saw in me a method of annoying his son, and the son saw in me the chance of ruining his father, and I was placed between two people greedy for unsavoury notoriety, reckless of anything except their own horrible hatred of each other. (*L* 414)

And he admitted:

The one disgraceful, unpardonable and to all time contemptible action of my life was allowing myself to be forced into appealing to Society for help and protection against your father. . . . Once I had put into motion the forces of Society, Society turned on me and said 'Have you been living all this time in defiance of my laws? You shall have those laws exercised to the full. You shall abide by what you have appealed to.' (*L* 491-2)

Wilde looked back on himself as a 'person of absurd good nature' and 'indescribable folly' (*L* 500), calling his prosecution of Queensberry 'a combination of absolute idiocy and vulgar bravado' (*L* 512) — probably the most perceptive comments he ever made about himself. He told Douglas:

I had always thought that my giving up to you in small things meant nothing: that when a great moment arrived I could reassert my will-power in its natural superiority. It was not so. At the great moment my will-power completely failed me. (*L* 430)

In order to rid himself of Queensberry, he and Douglas prepared to commit 'silly perjuries' (*L* 435), denying that there was any truth in Queensberry's allegations. To Douglas's surviving brother, who supported them morally and financially, they claimed that the accusation was the result of 'absurd and unaccountable delusions' on Queensberry's part (*L* 508), and in setting the prosecution on foot with Humphreys, the solicitor, they sat 'with serious faces telling serious lies to a bald man, till I nearly groaned and yawned with ennui' (*L* 493).

Wilde consulted a fortune-teller, Mrs Robinson, [100] 'the Sybil', on several occasions before his downfall. According to one authority, she told him: 'I see a very brilliant life for you up to a certain point. Then I see a wall. Beyond the wall I see nothing.' (*L* 358) She was not a particularly reliable clairvoyante, since she then 'prophesied complete triumph' (*L* 385) — at complete variance with 'Cheiro', who in his memoirs alleged that when he examined Wilde's hands on 20 February 1892 (the first night of *Lady Windermere's Fan*) he noticed the discrepancy between the left hand (hereditary tendencies) and the right (acquired). The left hand

> promised the most unusual destiny of brilliancy and uninterrupted success, which was completely broken and ruined at a certain date in the right; a being who will send himself into exile. 'At what date?' he asked rather quietly. 'A few years from now . . . between your forty-first and forty-second year.' ('Cheiro' 57)

('Cheiro' also alleged that at the Paris Exhibition of 1900 he prevented Wilde from drowning himself in the Seine.)

Constance Wilde also consulted 'the Sybil': 'What is to become of my husband who has so betrayed and deserted me and ruined the lives of my darling boys?. . . My life has all been cut to pieces as my hand is by its lines.' (*L* 389) ('You cut life to pieces with your epigrams,' Douglas once wrote to him.) She never succeeded in understanding Wilde's passions: 'He says that he loved too much, but this was an unnatural love, a madness that I think is worse than hate,' she wrote, and she refused to see him: 'Oscar is so pathetic and such a born actor. I am hardened when I am away from him.' (*L* 717, 718) She knew she could not resist the appeal from the child within him. 'Is happiness dead for me?' she asked. 'And I have had so little.' (*L* 389)

Queensberry was arrested on a charge of criminal libel on 2 March 1895 and brought before the magistrate in Great Marlborough Street, the proceedings being immediately adjourned and recommenced on 9 March. A prima facie case having been established, Queensberry was formally committed for trial on 3 April. Wilde and Douglas went off to Monte Carlo for a holiday, 'then return to fight with panthers' (*L* 384). They could not have realised how serious the fight would be. Queensberry had no evidence of sexual offences; it was assumed that Edward Carson, who had been briefed for the defence, would try to establish a plea of justification on the basis of Wilde's literary work – *Dorian Gray* in particular.

With the aid of private detectives and well-wishers, Queensberry rapidly assembled an astonishing dossier of Wilde's affairs, so that when the trial opened at the Old Bailey, at which another TCD man, Mr Justice Henn Collins, presided, he was equipped to demonstrate not only that Wilde was a poseur, but that he was also guilty of sexual offences.

One of the most frequently neglected references by Wilde to his guilt is his statement in 'De Profundis' that 'the sins of another' were being laid at his door (*L* 452). In view of the likelihood that on one key occasion (discussed above, p.80) the guilty party quite probably was Douglas, not Wilde, this claim must be taken seriously. It has been alleged that Queensberry's detectives uncovered a mass of evidence pointing to Douglas's own guilt and that Queensberry bribed his witnesses 'in the absolute transference, deliberate, plotted and rehearsed, of the actions and doings of someone else on to me' (*L* 452), not so much to punish Wilde as to save his son. However, Wilde himself agreed that he deserved punishment

since, although he may not have committed the
[102] actual offences alleged, he had committed others
equally serious:

> My record of perversities of passion and distorted
> romances would fill many scarlet volumes. . . .
> If a man gets drunk, whether he does so on white
> wine or red is of no importance. (*L* 515-16)

Wilde's unsuccessful prosecution of Queensberry
is chiefly remembered for the fact that Carson com-
bated Wilde's offensive frivolity and nonchalance
with a dogged persistence which was reinforced by
the fact that he held the trump cards — the witnesses
who were prepared to incriminate themselves as
Wilde's sexual partners. Wilde's attitude was certainly
damaging to himself. He answered flippantly and
casually, taking the opportunity to indulge his taste
for baiting conventional morality.

Carson and Wilde had met only once, briefly, since
their student days.[28] Until convinced of the nature of
Wilde's conduct Carson was reluctant to accept
Queensberry's brief. Now he found Wilde helping to
prove the Marquess's case by posing as something alien
and distasteful. An early indiscretion gave Carson an
opportunity to damage Wilde's credibility: the pro-
secutor gave his age as thirty-nine. Carson, his exact
contemporary, knew that Wilde was approaching his
forty-first birthday, and in cross-examination he
challenged him, forcing him to admit his true age:
'I have no wish to pose as being young.' (*T* 105)
Why did Wilde almost deliberately give Carson this
opening? Carson proceeded painstakingly to cross-
examine Wilde on two sonnets by Douglas, 'In Praise
of Shame' and 'Two Loves', passing on to his rejection
of morality in art, based on the temperament of
Dorian Gray. Wilde persistently attempted to put
himself beyond the reach of Carson and the court by

discounting his connection with social conventions:

'The affection and love of the artist of *Dorian Gray*
might lead an ordinary individual to believe that it
might have a certain tendency?'
'I have no knowledge of the views of ordinary
individuals.' (*T* 110)

He was also resolute in defending the artistic aspects
of Uranian love: 'I think it is perfectly natural for any
artist to admire intensely and love a young man.'
(*T* 112) Next Carson questioned Wilde on the 'prose
poem' letter he had written to Douglas referring to
his 'red rose-leaf lips' and 'slim gilt soul'. 'Was that
the ordinary way in which you carried on your correspondence?' 'Everything I write is extraordinary.'
(*T* 116-17) Carson, however, was beginning to get
inside Wilde's guard and to dismantle his defences:
'Is it the kind of letter a man writes to another?'
Wilde admitted that there had been an attempt
to blackmail him and that Taylor had introduced
him to about five young men with whom he afterwards became intimate, indignantly denying any
'immoral relations'. Carson proceeded to point out
markedly that these included a valet, a groom and a
bookmaker's tout, whom he took to Paris, as if
Wilde had broken a moral code simply by associating
with persons of that class. Wilde was forced to retort:

I delight in the society of people much younger
than myself. . . . I recognise no social distinctions
at all of any kind. . . . I would talk to a street arab
with pleasure. (*T* 129)

Wilde's flippancy tripped him up, however, as with
self-assurance he gave a truthful answer regarding one
of Douglas's men-servants: 'Did you ever kiss him?'
'Oh dear, no . . . he was unfortunately extremely
ugly.' (*T* 133) This admission, out of place but not

out of character, shocked the court, and it was clear
that Carson had succeeded in damaging his opponent's credibility. In re-examination Wilde's counsel, Sir Edward Clarke, tried to repair the damage, but the most unfavourable impression had been created in an already hostile courtroom. In fact the court was only 'with' Wilde when he was amusing them temporarily at Carson's expense, for example: 'Strictly against my doctor's orders.' 'Never mind your doctor's orders.' 'I never do.' (*T* 129) Only Queensberry's offensive character and the reading of his letters in which he verbally assaulted his family and Wilde, even questioning his sons' legitimacy, mitigated Wilde's real plight. Clarke closed the case for the prosecution.

When Carson opened for the defence, having characterised Taylor's rooms as 'a shameful den', and alleged that 'Taylor has in fact been the right-hand man of Mr Wilde in all the orgies in which artists and valets have taken part', he said: 'It will be painful to be compelled to ask the various witnesses that will be called, to describe the manner in which Mr Wilde has acted towards them.' (*T* 142) The court realised that Queensberry had persuaded Wilde's partners to incriminate themselves by admitting to illegal sexual practices with him. Carson also saved the day for Douglas by absolving him from these affairs: 'I am not here to say anything has ever happened between Lord Alfred Douglas and Mr Oscar Wilde. God forbid!' (*T* 143)

In consultation that evening Clarke told his client that if he allowed the case to run on, and the jury acquitted Queensberry, the judge would almost certainly order Wilde's immediate arrest. Wilde agreed to withdraw the prosecution. Clarke recalled: 'I hoped and expected that he would take the opportunity of escaping from the country, and I believe

that he would have found no difficulty in doing so.'
(*T* 145) Wilde had jokingly said, years before, that he
would get twenty-four hours' grace in the event of a
warrant for his arrest. There was in fact a delay
between the application to the Bow Street magistrate
for a warrant for Wilde's arrest, at 3.30 p.m. on 5
April, and its issue after 5 p.m., by which time
Wilde could have been on the boat-train. However,
according to one biographer, the Home Secretary had
already given instructions that 'wherever Wilde might
be found he should be stopped' (Hyde 224). Carson
is said to have gone home sadly and told his wife: 'I
have ruined the most brilliant man in London.'[29]

Wilde lost his nerve. Waiting for the inevitable
arrest, he wrote a letter to the *Evening News* intended
as a cover-up:

> It would have been impossible for me to have
> proved my case without putting Lord Alfred
> Douglas in the witness-box against his father. . . .
> Rather than put him in so painful a position I
> determined to retire from the case. (*L* 386)

Douglas could not have given evidence, because he
had no admissible evidence to give.[30] This unnecessary
attempt at dignity therefore shows that Wilde's
judgment was faulty.

*   *   *

Wilde was arrested at the Cadogan Hotel at
6.30 p.m. on 5 April. He was formally charged under
Section 11 of the Criminal Law Amendment Act,
1885,[31] on twenty-five counts of gross indecency with
various male persons on and after 20 March 1893,
and was taken to Bow Street police station, where, on
being searched, he was found to have £200 in £5
notes, writs for payment on cigarette cases and other
items, and a letter from Taylor referring to police

surveillance. Taylor was also arrested, and they were
[106] both committed for trial on 19 April. Bail was not
allowed.

The *Daily Chronicle* (6 April) said:

> There was one centre whence a most deadly
> infection spread; it was apparent in a certain class
> of literature.... 'Decadence' among us has received
> a death-blow. ... Essentially right and inevitable
> tendencies in art and in literature have been foully
> prostituted.

The *Daily Telegraph* referred to Wilde's 'spurious
brilliancy, inflated egotism, diseased vanity, cultured
affectation and shameless disavowal of all morality'.
Carson had exposed the pagan 'cynicism, scepticism
and animalism' which Wilde had introduced into
'healthy and honest English art and life'. At last Wilde
was detected in trying, as he said of his poem *The
Sphinx*, to 'destroy domesticity in England'. Henley's
National Observer congratulated Queensberry

> for destroying the High Priest of the Decadents.
> The obscene imposter, whose prominence has been
> a social outrage ever since he transferred from
> Trinity Dublin to Oxford his vices, his follies and
> his vanities, has been exposed. ... There must be
> legal and social sequels ... another trial ... or a
> coroner's inquest — the latter for choice.

One telegram to Queensberry read 'Every man in the
City is with you. Kill the bugger!' (Hyde 228) Henley
wrote:

> Yes: Oscar at bay was, on the whole, a pleasing
> sight. The air is alive with rumours, of course; but
> I believe no new arrests will be made, and that
> morality will be satisfied if Oscar gets two years;
> as of course he will. Why he didn't stay at Monte
> Carlo, once he got there, God alone knows. Seeing

that . . . he returned to face the music, and play the Roman fool to Caesar's Destiny, I can only conjecture that, what between personal and professional vanity, he was stark mad. (Connell, 298-9)

As Wilde's first trial came to a conclusion William Archer wrote:

I'm afraid Oscar hasn't the ghost of a chance. . . . He's practically a dead man on his own admission in the previous trial. It is a loathsome and unthinkable business, but certainly Oscar's madness is not inconsistent with an extraordinary courage and nerve. . . . Really the luck is against the poor British drama — the man who has more brains in his little finger than all the rest of them in their whole body goes and commits worse than suicide in this way. (Archer 215)

Henry James wrote to Gosse of the 'squalid tragedy', which he found 'hideously, atrociously dramatic and really interesting' with a 'sickening horribility' (Edel II 187). Queensberry himself wrote to the *Star:*

Were I the authority that had to mete out to him his punishment I would treat him with all possible consideration as a sexual pervert of utterly diseased mind, not as a sane criminal. If it is sympathy Mr Wilde has it from me to this extent.

While a conviction was generally expected, the point must be made that in fact some of the evidence against Wilde was flimsy. The jury was largely being asked to convict on the basis of the uncorroborated evidence of self-confessed accomplices. But the weight of public opinion was so heavy that the prosecution had no alternative but to press on as hard as possible. Douglas's cousin, George Wyndham, MP, told him that the government had urged a 'satisfactory' conclusion to a case which involved 'the systematic

ruin of a number of young men' (Hyde 231), thus
[108] covering up the government's real anxiety that the
scandal had mentioned the name of the Prime Minister,
that the nephew by marriage of the Solicitor-General
was one of Wilde's boys, that Balfour himself had
been amicably associated with the Wildes, and that
Wilde's plays had been openly admired by the Prince
of Wales. As André Raffalovich pointed out in
L'Affaire Oscar Wilde which he hastily published in
Paris:

> When I say he has a criminal nature, I am not con-
> cerned with the sexual offences with which he has
> been charged, but with the role he has played,
> the influence he has exerted, with the young
> ideas he has misdirected, the vices he has advoc-
> ated. English society is equally to blame. [My
> translation]

In a direct comparison with the Cleveland Street
scandal he pointed out that in that case the details

> proved that private vices made use of a recog-
> nised system.... One cannot accuse society of
> unwarranted tolerance nor the guilty parties of
> wanting to practice sodomy openly.... Sodom
> exists, venal and menacing, the invisible city. But
> the 'Oscar Wilde tragedy' is of another kind. Oscar
> Wilde has been encouraged, tolerated by English
> society. He was regarded as an institution.

Wilde had made visible 'the invisible city' and had
presented the shocked bourgeoisie, in the most offensive possible manner, with proof of a widespread
culture of *paederasteia* and homoerotism. Thus the
fault seemed to be as much in the double standards
of the day whereby Wilde was kept as a fashionable
plaything while he amused, as in Wilde the saboteur
of public morals.

Wilde's personal fortunes declined rapidly. Willie (or perhaps even Lady Wilde) was seen piling luggage into a cab in Tite Street, and both Constance and Ross attempted to remove as much of value as they could. However, they seem to have been powerless to prevent a creditors' auction held on the premises, at which the entire remaining contents, including Wilde's library, his blue and white china and the children's toys, were sold at a fraction of their value. At the same time his name was removed from the playbills at the theatres where *An Ideal Husband* and *The Importance of Being Earnest* were running (they were soon taken off completely), and his books were withdrawn from the bookshops.

*   *   *

Wilde faced his trial on 26 April 1895, with Mr Justice Charles on the bench. Clarke defended him; Charles Gill (an Ulsterman) prosecuted. Wilde and Taylor were jointly indicted on a total of twenty-five counts. Clarke immediately objected on procedural grounds to the joint indictment, but was overruled. Gill's opening speech showed the deliberate course the prosecution intended to take: 'This youth [Atkins] accompanied the prisoner Wilde to Paris, and there can be no doubt whatever that the prisoner endeavoured in the most systematic way to influence the young man's mind towards vicious courses and endeavoured to mould him to his own depraved will.' (*T* 169) Not only did Gill draw out the facts of the alleged indecencies, but he also put them in the context of the 'seductions', the dinners and champagne, use of women's clothes in Taylor's house, the gifts of jewellery, all likely to shock and prejudice the jury.

Clarke decided to call Wilde in his own defence. He prefaced his case by saying that his client had brought the prosecution on himself through his action against

Queensberry and had no doubt as to the nature of the evidence against him now. It was during cross-examination by Gill that Wilde made the speech which stands as his only complete public defence of Uranian love, and which did much to confuse and unsettle the jury, as it impressed almost the whole court. Gill asked Wilde: 'What is the "love that dare not speak its name"?', to which Wilde replied:

> 'The love that dare not speak its name' in this century is such a great affection of an older for a younger man as there was between David and Jonathan, such as Plato made the very basis of his philosophy, and such as you find in the sonnets of Michaelangelo and Shakespeare. It is that deep, spiritual affection that is as pure as it is perfect. It dictates and pervades great works of art. . . . It is in this century misunderstood, so much misunderstood that it may be described as the 'love that dare not speak its name' and on account of it I am placed where I am now. It is beautiful, it is fine, it is the noblest form of affection. There is nothing unnatural about it. It is intellectual, and it repeatedly exists between an elder and a younger man, when the elder has intellect, and the younger man has all the joy, hope, and glamour of life before him. That it should be so, the world does not understand. The world mocks at it, and sometimes puts one in the pillory for it. (T 201)

This unashamed admission and unequivocal claim met with spontaneous applause in court. Gill's summing up for the Crown typified the feelings of the anti-decadents and the government:

> You owe a duty to society, however sorry you may feel yourselves at the moral downfall of an eminent man, to protect society from such scandals by

removing from its heart a sore which cannot fail in time to corrupt and taint it all. (*T* 213) [111]

In contrast, Clarke offered the jury the opportunity to 'clear society from a stain' by dismissing preconceptions and rejecting the spurious evidence it had heard. The judge's direction to the jury was impartial, stressing the need in case of doubt to give the benefit to the defendants. He observed not only that the evidence of accomplices must be corroborated, but also that as blackmailers their characters should be taken into consideration. It was touch and go. After nearly four hours the jury failed to reach a verdict, and a retrial was ordered. Next day, 3 May, Wilde was released on bail of £5,000, put up by well-wishers.

Determined to secure a conviction, the Crown now put the fresh prosecution in the hands of the Solicitor-General himself, Sir Frank Lockwood. Carson remonstrated: 'Cannot you let up on the fellow now? He has suffered a great deal.' But because of the names mentioned it was essential to pursue the matter. Shaw and Harris urged Wilde to jump bail – Douglas's brother said he would honour the sureties. Wilde refused. On 20 May 1895 he surrendered his bail at the Old Bailey, and on 22 May once more stood trial. Taylor was tried first and was found guilty.

Of the eight remaining counts, four related to acts of gross indecency with Charles Parker (formerly a valet, now a soldier and prostitute) at the Savoy Hotel, at St James's Place and elsewhere; two to offences with other (unknown) persons at the Savoy Hotel; one to an offence with Alfred Wood (clerk and blackmailer) at Tite Street; and one in relation to Edward Shelley (clerk at John Lane's). Clarke dealt devastatingly with much of the evidence from witnesses at the Savoy Hotel, and in reply to his submission

that there was no case to answer in respect of the
[112] Savoy Hotel, the judge almost agreed ('The point . . .
is just on the line') but inexplicably he decided
that although 'it would not be fair . . . that a
number of nothings should be put to make up something, I think, however, on the whole the wiser and
safer course would be to allow the count . . . to go
to the jury' (*T* 238-9). On the other hand, he agreed
to the withdrawal of the count relating to Shelley.

Lockwood repeated Carson's and Gill's incredulous
attitude to Wilde's lack of social bias: 'What pleasure
can you find in the society of boys much beneath
you in social position?' (*T* 248) He carried this into
his devastating closing speech for the Crown:

> He is a man of culture and literary tastes, and I
> submit that his associates ought to have been his
> equals and not these illiterate boys whom you
> have heard in the witness-box. (*T* 255)

In his summing up Mr Justice Wills tipped the
scales against Wilde. While there was nothing in his
address which could have been referred to a court
of appeal, he proposed not to give Wilde the benefit
of the doubt. He echoed an earlier note:

> There is some truth in the aphorism that a man
> must be judged by the company he keeps. Are
> these the kind of young men with whom you your-
> selves would care to sit down and dine? (*T* 266-7)

The evidence was discussed in detail. The jury retired
for over two hours, before returning to find Wilde
guilty on all counts. Citing Wilde as undoubtedly 'the
centre of a circle of extensive corruption of the most
hideous kind among young men' (*T* 272), Mr Justice
Wills sentenced him to the maximum of two years
with hard labour.

Wilde had dreamed of elevating aesthetics above

ethics, which the Victorian code disallowed. He was punished because, while the Cleveland Street scandal had shown that throughout society 'the Hellenic ideal' could incite men physically Wilde had shown that it could excite their minds.

2
In Carcere et Vinculis

Wilde spent his imprisonment first at Pentonville and later at Wandsworth and Reading. He was taken, already shattered by the realisation of his complete eclipse, to Pentonville on 27 May 1895, weighed and measured (he was six feet tall and weighed slightly less than fourteen stone — hardly gross for a man of large build), bathed, given a convict uniform and locked in a cell measuring sixteen feet by seven, and nine feet high, to which he was confined for twenty-three hours each day. After six months Haldane told Henry James that Wilde was 'in a state of complete dejection, physical and moral' and had no capacity for recovery (Edel II 194). He had lost two stone by this stage, and the deprivations of prison had greatly impaired his mental and physical balance. The only occasions when he left prison were on 24 September and 12 November 1895, to attend Queensberry's final triumph, the public examination in the Bankruptcy Court, mainly brought about by his obligation to pay Queensberry's costs (£677) in the aborted libel action.

In the middle of his imprisonment Wilde petitioned for clemency on clinical grounds, begging relief not only from his almost total solitary confinement but also from the lack of writing materials and reading matter (two books each week from the small prison library) and from the physical conditions which caused deterioration in hearing and eyesight, 'an

existence composed of bitter degradations and terrible
[114] hardships' in 'this tomb for those who are not yet
dead' (*L* 403). He asked unsuccessfully that he might
'be taken abroad ... and put himself under medical
care so that the sexual insanity from which he suffers
may be cured' (*L* 404). Referring to the 'intimate
connection between madness and the literary and
artistic temperament', he admitted:

> While the three years preceding his arrest were
> from the intellectual point of view the most
> brilliant years of his life ... during the entire time
> he was suffering from the most horrible form of
> erotomania, which made him forget his wife and
> children, his high social position in London and
> Paris, his European distinction as an artist, the
> honour of his name and family, his very humanity
> itself, and left him the helpless prey of the most
> revolting passions. (*L* 402)

Six months later Wilde petitioned again for an early
release, once more to be rejected. The Home Office,
however, requisitioned a report from specialists at
Broadmoor who recommended some mitigation of
the solitary confinement but observed that 'It would
not be right to allow a man with his proclivities and
with his avowed love for the society of males to be in
association *except with the continuous supervision of
a warder*.' (Hyde, *Aftermath* 37, official emphasis)

Wilde knew now that he had been living a life
'unworthy of an artist', a life of 'gilded infamy ...
Neronian ... rich, profligate, cynical, materialistic'
(*L* 577). After a year in prison he had come to hate
Douglas, and to be shamed by the memory of his
association with him, while developing a strong
psychological dependence on Ross, to whom he wrote:

> I wish to be certain that he [Douglas] has in his

possession nothing that I ever gave him. . . . The
idea that he is wearing or is in possession of any- [115]
thing I gave him is peculiarly repugnant to me. I
cannot of course get rid of the revolting memories
of the two years I was unlucky enough to have him
with me, and of the mode by which he thrust me
into the abyss of ruin and disgrace to gratify his
hatred of his father and other ignoble passions.
(*L* 400-1)

As a form of purgation, a therapy, with Douglas as
the unwitting catalyst, he wrote an astonishing letter,
which he began in January 1897 and completed over
a three-month period, in which he analysed his
relationship with his lover, his own character and
personality, the features of the age in which he lived,
his relationship to the age, and his world-view from
the heights compared with his new perspective 'de
profundis'. Given that the letter displays all the
phobia of a brilliant man incarcerated in a very
oppressive place, all the petulance and grievance of
a born invert and egotist, and all the attitudinising of
a confirmed poseur, 'De Profundis', originally intended
to be entitled 'Epistola in Carcere et Vinculis', is a
self-analysis of great force, a love-letter of humility
as well as of charm and charity, and a social document
of relevance both to Wilde's condition at the time of
writing and to the situation of the 'outsider' or
'antinomian'.

Wilde has been criticised for regarding prison as his
personal Calvary. This was not, however, an *ad hoc*
viewpoint — he had conceived it in 1889 when reviewing Wilfrid Scawen Blunt's *In Vinculis*. Blunt had
written: 'Imprisonment is a reality of discipline most
useful to the *modern soul*, lapped as it is in physical
sloth and self-indulgence. Like a sickness or a spiritual
retreat it purifies and ennobles.' (*AC* 116, my emphasis)
This helps to explain Wilde's trick of universalising

and at the same time personalising all his emotions and
[116] characteristics, and his identification with two great
'romantic failures', Napoleon and Christ. So he wrote
himself big, referring to himself in Christlike terms:

> One of the most wonderful things in the whole of
> recorded time: the crucifixion of the Innocent One
> before the eyes of his mother and of the disciple
> whom he loved. (*L* 478: i.e. Speranza and Ross)

He justified his personal creed in terms of Christ's
teaching:

> When he says 'Forgive your enemies' it is not for the
> sake of the enemy but for one's own sake. (*L* 480)

The argument sounds suspiciously like Sir Robert
Chiltern's belief that temptation is something one
must have courage to yield to. Wilde makes Christ the
scapegoat for his own epigrams:

> For him there were no laws, there were exceptions
> merely. (*L* 485).

> Out of his own imagination entirely did Jesus of
> Nazareth create himself. (*L* 482)

'I don't write this letter to put bitterness into your
heart,' he told Douglas, 'but to pluck it out of mine.'
(*L* 465) Reviewing his life, he realised that he had
lived only for pleasure, which he did not regret for a
single moment, but he had been afraid of 'failure,
disgrace, poverty, sorrow, despair, suffering . . . pain,
remorse, self-abasement' (*L* 475). With the disdain of
reason from his Oxford days, he tried to find some
grounds for rehabilitation in a society whose laws he
had rejected: 'Reason does not help me. It tells me
that the laws under which I am convicted are wrong
and unjust laws' (*L* 468): 'the terrible squealing of
the slaughtered pig', as Lawrence Durrell called it
(*Black Book* 49).

He intended to discuss with Douglas 'our ill-fated and most lamentable friendship' (*L* 424) which he now decided had been intellectually degrading: 'You were the absolute ruin of my art.' (*L* 427) Douglas's faults, he concluded, were congenital. Mr Justice Wills had called the family 'a house divided against itself'; Wilde called it a family 'marriage to whom is horrible, friendship fatal, and which lays violent hands, either on its own life or on the lives of others' (*L* 440). It was Douglas's aristocratic disdain for life, his profligate recklessness, his 'unrestrained and coarse appetites' which, he told Ross, repulsed him: 'I blame him for not appreciating the man he ruined.' (*L* 413) However, Wilde's claim in 'De Profundis' for his lost social and artistic position becomes laughable:

I, once the lord of language. . . (*L* 458)

I was to many an arbiter of style in Art. (*L* 462)

. . . that beautiful unreal world of Art where once I was King (*L* 463)

The gods had given me almost everything. I had genius, a distinguished name, high social position, brilliancy, intellectual daring. (*L* 466)

Whatever I touched I made beautiful in a new mode of beauty. . . . I awoke the imagination of my century. . . penning comedies that were to beat Congreve for brilliancy, and Dumas *fils* for philosophy. (*L* 500)

Despite the rigour and demoralisation of prison life, Wilde's incarceration was not as utterly miserable as we might think. He succeeded in exercising a childlike attraction which found some sympathy with the warders and the governor of Reading prison, Major Nelson. One warder saw in him 'just a bundle of brains — and that is all' (*IR* 328). Moreover, special conditions were established for his reading: he had access to, among other writers, Pater, St Augustine, Pascal, Mommsen (the *History of Rome*), Newman, Dante and collections of the Greek and Latin poets. Later he received a Greek Testament, Tennyson, Keats, Chaucer, Renan and other French authors ('The chaplain has no objection to these if they are in the original French,' says an official report), Ranke's *History of the Popes*, Milman's *History of the Jews* and a collected edition of Dickens. Huysmans' *En Route* was disallowed. He also seems to have received private presents of books, which were presumably vetted by the prison authorities, and he was able to purchase books which he presented to the prison library, including Wordsworth, Arnold, Dryden, Burns, Dante, Chaucer, Milman, Buckle, Goethe, Goldoni, Pater, Rossetti and a selection of dictionaries.

During Wilde's imprisonment Constance was concerned with the eventual custody of her children and her relationship with her husband on his release. Finally a separation was arranged whereby Wilde relinquished all claim to his children in return for an annual allowance of £150, provided he committed no moral misdemeanour and did not consort with 'evil and disreputable persons'. Constance actually met her husband for the last time when, on Speranza's death on 3 February 1896, she travelled from Italy, where she was living, to give him the news. Discussing the deed of arrangement, Wilde wrote to Ross, who was increasingly taking on his business affairs:

Whether I am married or not is a matter that does not concern me. For years I disregarded the tie. But I really think that it is hard on my wife to be tied to me. I always thought so. And, though it might surprise some of my friends, I am really very fond of my wife and very sorry for her. . . . She could not understand me, and I was bored to death with married life. But she had some sweet points in her character, and was wonderfully loyal to me. (*L* 516)

One pathetic aspect of this displacement as a person, his loss — or abandonment — of respectability, was his genuine inconsolable despair at the removal of his sons:

I sincerely hope I may be recognised by the Court as having some little, I won't say right, but claim to be allowed to see Cyril from time to time: it would be to me a sorrow beyond words if I were not. I do hope the Court will see in me something more than a man with a tragic vice in his life. There is so much more in me, and I always was a good father to both my children. I love them dearly and was dearly loved by them, and Cyril was my friend. (*L* 422)

At first Constance wrote to him every week, but despite several attempts, after his release, to effect a reunion, even a temporary visit to his sons, Wilde never saw them again, although they were allowed to send their photographs and 'remembrances' to their father.

3
The Slippery Pavement of Paris

In Reading Wilde faced 'the horror of death with the still greater horror of living' (*L* 400). 'Horrible as are the dead when they rise from their tombs, the living who come out from tombs are more horrible still.' (*L* 413) On 19 May 1897 he was released (from Pentonville, the prison to which he had been originally committed) to face the horror of living. He had little self-regard, except as 'a man with a tragic vice in his life'.

He decided to adopt the pseudonym 'Sebastian Melmoth' — a composite identity of the saint transfixed with arrows (like his own prison costume) and the wandering hero of Maturin's Gothic fantasy who declared: 'I have been on earth a terror, but not an evil to its inhabitants.' Wilde believed that 'I shall return an unwelcome visitant to the world that does not want me; a revenant ... as one whose face is grey with long imprisonment and crooked with pain.' (L 413)

Ada Leverson, meeting him in London on the morning of his release, thought that he looked 'markedly better, slighter and younger than he had two years previously'. She was one of the few friends courageous enough to acknowledge him. But he immediately encountered the coldness which many of his former associates would display in the next three years. One of his most steadfast friends, Reggie Turner, wrote (with obvious relief) that he would be unable to meet him in England, but would see him in France: 'Were my presence to be made known by any means to my people, my allowance would be stopped.' (L 557) That evening Wilde crossed from Newhaven to Dieppe, where he was met by Ross and Turner: 'I have thought it better that Robbie should stay here under the name of Reginald Turner, and Reggie under the name of R. B. Ross. It is better that they should not have their own names.' (L 566)[32]

Shortly before his release Wilde had become obsessed with business matters relating to his marriage and provision for his future life. Constance would not communicate with him directly, the intervening solicitors became unhelpful, and friends seemed to bungle affairs. From his cell Wilde thought he saw the situation with great clarity and lucidity, and his letters, presumably because of the mounting obsession with money which dominated his imagination for the rest of his life, show a great perspicacity. As a result of his imprisonment everyone else becomes a traitor, a rogue or a fool. Of the correspondence with his two greatest supporters in prison, Ross and More Adey, 'the best title would be *Letters from two idiots to a lunatic*' (*L* 550). As he prepared to meet Ross on embarking from England, he telegraphed ahead with a strong sense of self-preservation: 'You must not mind the foolish unkind letters.' (*L* 565) Reggie Turner tried to persuade him that 'When you come to talk over what has been done for you, you will see that all has been done in the best way when one remembers the terrible difficult position. . . . Try to be patient, try in this time, so terrible for your nerves, to be yourself, great, wonderful, noble.' (*L* 557)

'Dear Robbie, so thoughtful for others, is making arrangements for me to live in a cheerful French pension, with table d'hôte at 6.30 and pleasant ladies' society in the evenings. I am to play dominoes.' (*L* 681) Wilde and Ross had a love-hate correspondence for the next three years, Wilde alternately berating and cajoling, wooing and entreating: 'You are made to help me.' (*L* 577) Wilde had no earning capacity and, apart from his meagre allowance, relied on the generosity of friends and admirers to keep a tenuous hold on life: 'There is no such thing as changing one's life, one merely wanders round and round within the circle of one's own personality.' (*L* 671) He acknowledged gratefully, if remorsefully, the attempts to do 'the best thing for him', 'to create a possible life for me', but he could not accede to the preconditions: 'You know what beautiful, wise, sensible schemes of life people bring to one. There is nothing to be said against them; except that they are not for oneself.' (*L* 673)

Believing that his friends would establish a 'deposit fund' for his use on release, Wilde had planned to live quietly and anonymously for the first eighteen months while he reconstructed his life. No such fund ever existed. The disappointment was acute because in prison he had pictured an ideal life of retreat and

comfort, 'as a man of letters should have — that is
[122] with a private sitting-room and books and the like. I
can see no other way of living, if I am to write,
though I can see many others, if I am not.' (*L* 588-9)
In fact he was not; the private sitting-room was most
often a dingy adjunct to a seedy bedroom, mainly
without books. For a man of such exaggerated
aspirations it was not unreasonable to expect some
recompense, particularly from Douglas, who promised something:

> Bosie is anxious to make 'some little return' to me
> for all 'I spent on him'. Unfortunately I spent on
> him my life, my genius, my position, my name in
> history; for these no little or big return is possible.
> (*L*421-2)

After a few days in the vicinity of Dieppe Wilde
found lodgings at a nearby village, Berneval-sur-Mer.
He easily tired of a place, as he tired of a boy. At
first Berneval was a paradise: 'I adore this place, the
whole country is lovely. . . . It is simple and healthy. . . .
If I lived in the South of Italy I know I should be idle,
and worse. I want to live here.' (*L* 585) After a brief
reunion with Douglas his attitude changed completely:
'I cannot stay in the North of Europe; the climate
kills me. . . . My last fortnight at Berneval has been
black and dreadful, and quite suicidal. I have never
been so unhappy. I am trying to get some money to
go to Italy.' (*L* 638)

He began to write *The Ballad of Reading Gaol*, the
memorial to an unknown Othello who suffered the
ultimate penalty of a brutal law. The *Ballad* is a flawed
masterpiece. Wilde uses a traditionally lyrical medium
(Speranza's *Thelka* of 1861 should be considered an
inspiration) as a propaganda vehicle. As a literary
memorial it reads well, emotively, but as an exercise
in elocution the language is only partially successful.

Despite its subsequent popular appeal, Wilde and Ross had difficulties in finding a publisher — both had doubts as to its merits. 'The poem suffers under the difficulty of a divided aim in style. Some is realistic, some is romantic: some poetry, some propaganda,' Wilde wrote. (*L* 654) Besides the problem of the ballad's suitability for Wilde's purposes, there were technical difficulties. Wilde had assumed that troopers' uniforms were scarlet, and had written: 'He did not wear his scarlet coat / For blood and wine are red' (*W* 843), but when it was pointed out to him that the regiment wore blue tunics he proposed to amend the lines to read: 'He did not wear his azure coat / For blood and wine are blue' (*L* 730).

Wilde had left prison determined never to see Douglas: 'To be with him would be to return to the hell from which I do think I have been released. I hope never to see him again.' (*L* 577) But within a month of his arrival in France he was corresponding, although cautiously, with Douglas. At first he resisted a meeting: 'Of course I love you more than anyone else [i.e. more than Ross]. But our lives are irreparably severed, as far as meeting goes.' (*L* 595). This was written on 4 June; on 16 June he invited Douglas to meet him three days later, instructing him to bring from Paris a bathing-costume, books, cigarettes, a straw hat and flannels (*L* 610-11). On the following day he put off the meeting because he received a notification from his solicitors, creating 'apprehension of serious danger', i.e. cessation of his allowance if he lived with Douglas and the threat of renewed pursuit by Queensberry. 'Later on,' he told Douglas, 'when the alarm in England is over, when secrecy is possible, and silence forms part of the world's attitude, we may meet' (*L* 613), and he reassured Ross: 'A.D. is not here, nor is he to come.' Finally they met at the end of August at Rouen. Within a couple of days Wilde wrote:

My only hope of again doing beautiful work in art is being with you. It was not so in the old days, but now it is different. . . . Everyone is furious with me for going back to you, but they don't understand us. (*L* 637)

'Yes, I saw Bosie,' he admitted to Ross, 'and of course I love him as I always did, with a sense of tragedy and ruin.' (*L* 638) As he headed south to rejoin Douglas in Italy he wrote to Ross: 'My only hope of life or literary activity was in going back to the young man I loved before.' (*L* 645) He also said that if Constance had permitted him to see his sons he might have acted differently. After four months she did send an invitation to see her, but the children were specifically excluded. Wilde declined.

Wilde's justification is typical of the child in him, to have the thing he wanted, and to be wanted in return, and also of the social victim, determined to show that punishment has not taken away his illicit prize:

I cannot live without the atmosphere of love: I must love and be loved, whatever price I pay for it. I could have lived all my life with you [Ross] but you have other claims on you. . . . When people speak against me for going back to Bosie, tell them that he offered me love, and that in my loneliness and disgrace I, after three months' struggle against a hideous Philistine world, returned naturally to him. Of course I shall often be unhappy, but still I love him; the mere fact that he wrecked my life makes me love him. (*L* 644)

My romance is a tragedy, of course, but it is none the less a romance. (*L* 648)

To Reggie Turner he wrote after one month with Douglas: 'Of course he is unchanged . . . still the same wilful, fascinating, irritating, destructive, delightful, personality.' (L 658) In fact in this attitude Wilde provides an index to the behaviour and mental dis- position of his last years: total disillusion with his own achievements as a personality; resignation to oblivion, after a penurious and shameful eclipse; and defiance towards a society from which, on his own admission, he had invited his punishment. It is ironic that we know more about his movements in the last three years of his life than of any other period except his year in America. The sentiment which emerges from his last letters is that of a man for whom life holds no mysteries, no pretence and no hope. In this phase Wilde ceased to pose, and only cheap glimpses of his earlier personality survive.

In Naples Wilde and Douglas were ostracised by the English colony, but 'fortunately we have a few simple friends among the poorer classes' (L 653). They also visited Taormina, meeting Baron von Gloeden, the photographer of Sicilian youths in 'classical poses'.

Constance and Lady Queensberry both reacted predictably, and Wilde and Douglas lost their allowances. Constance called Douglas 'that appalling individual' (L 653), apparently deciding on the advice of the jealous Ross, who thus succeeded in breaking up the Naples ménage, that Douglas was a 'disreputable person'. She wrote to her husband: 'I forbid you to return to your filthy, insane life. . . . What am I to think of you if you still have intercourse with your infamous companions?' (L 681) Constance recommenced the allowance — paid through Ross — when Wilde moved to Paris and was proved to be living completely apart from Douglas. According to Wilde, Douglas left him when the money ran out: 'He became terrible, unkind, mean and penurious, except where his own pleasures were concerned.' (L 709-10)

Constance Wilde had once more contemplated

divorce, apparently on the basis of fresh evidence of
other sexual offences, and it was said that Sir George
Lewis had agreed to act for her (see *L* 547), but she
seemed satisfied with the separation. Very close to
the end of her life she had been preparing for a recon-
ciliation, overcoming the 'absolute repulsion' which
she had developed (Hyde 339). Her brother also
believed that 'it will prove that she is acting for the
best in taking him back' (*L* 872), but her final illness
prevented this. She died in Genoa in April 1898 aged
forty. 'Oscar did not feel it at all,' Ross callously and
untruthfully said. (*L* 729)

Left to his own resources, Wilde drifted aimlessly
wherever he could find cheap accommodation and
temporary relief. In Italy he found that 'I can live for
ten francs a day (boy compris).' (*L* 791) He told Ross:

> As regards my marrying again, I am quite sure that
> you will want me to marry this time some sensible,
> practical, plain, middle-aged boy, and I don't like
> the idea at all. Besides I am practically engaged to
> a fisherman of extraordinary beauty, age eighteen.
> (*L* 775)

Max Beerbohm reported that Wilde was 'under surveillance by the French police [he had been warned
not to cause a scandal, under threat of deportation],
I suppose he is playing the giddy goat' (Cecil 123).
In 1897 *Le Jour* stated that in Paris Wilde's name was
synonymous with 'pathologie passionnelle' (*L* 589).

At the end of 1898 Wilde went (apparently at
Frank Harris's expense) to Napoule near Cannes,
where he met Harold Mellor, an unbalanced wealthy
young Englishman — 'sent away from Harrow at the
age of fourteen for being loved by the captain of the
cricket team' (*L* 775) — who was prepared to take
him to Switzerland and give him champagne. But
soon, characteristically, he tired of Mellor and

Switzerland — 'a rather dreadful combination' (*L* 785). From 'charming' Mellor becomes a 'silent, dull person, cautious and economical' (*L* 786). He found the Swiss ugly and longed for the beautiful Italian youths they had enjoyed: Eolo ('his father . . . sold him to Harold for 200 lire': *L* 775), Andre, Didaco ('a face chiselled for high romance': *L* 787), Pietro ('like a young St John. One would have followed him into the desert': *L* 776). Eventually Ross brought him back to Paris, from where, with the exception of a remarkable visit to Rome and Palermo, he scarcely emerged.

On 'the slippery pavement of Paris', as Baudelaire's step-father had called it, Wilde cruised and indulged his cruder tastes, investing them with a poetic flavour they seldom offered. In his letters to England he catalogues the boys: Henri, Edouarde, 'Casquette', Maurice Gilbert (a constant companion) — 'How is my golden Maurice?' he asked when he sent him over to London as a treat to amuse Ross and Turner; 'I suppose he is wildly loved? His upper lip is more like a rose-leaf than any other rose-leaf I ever saw' (*L* 739) — 'a young Russian called Maltchek Perovinski', a 'young poet, Michel Robas', Gaston, Eugene ('the harvest moon, the prize melon', i.e. uncircumcised), Léon, Georges ('a most passionate faun . . . eyes like the night and a scarlet flower of a mouth': *L* 765), Marius, Joseph, Alphonse and Edmond ('de Goncourt', Douglas's boy-friend, also called 'Florifer'). 'My companions are such as I can get, and I of course have to pay for such friendships, though I am bound to say they are not exigeants or expensive.' (*L* 740)

Few friends acknowledged Wilde or sought him in Paris. Work became more and more remote. He hoped for continental respectability, for example through an Italian translation of *Dorian Gray*: 'I want the Italians to realise that there has been more to my life

than a love for Narcissus or a passion for Sporus,
fascinating though both may be.' (*L* 695) At the end
of 1897 there was a chance of Eleanora Duse playing
Salome, but nothing came of it. Apart from *The
Ballad of Reading Gaol*, Wilde produced nothing but
promises. Wyndham discussed the adaptation of
Dumas's *La Dame de Monsorban* and Scribe's *Le
Verre d'Eau*, and Heinemann an introduction to
Maeterlinck's *La Princesse Maleine*, but without result.
He still felt under an obligation to complete plays for
Alexander and Wyndham which he had started before
his imprisonment, and when Augustin Daly asked
him for a play he replied that if there were anything
in him the two English theatre managers should have
the prior claim: 'If I took your money I know I
would simply have to return it in three months.'
(*L* 634) In the September after his release he intended
to rewrite his *Florentine Tragedy*, but as regards the
sort of play which had made his reputation, 'I simply
have no heart to write clever comedy' (*L* 639); 'My
sense of humour is now concentrated on the
grotesqueness of tragedy' (*L* 659); 'I have pleasures
and passions, but the joy of life is gone.' (*L* 708) He
regarded the *Ballad* as his *'chant de cygne'* (*L* 715).

In the case of Frank Harris, who wanted to buy
the scenario (written in 1894) of *Mr and Mrs Daventry*,
there were serious problems because Wilde had sold it
to at least six other concerns. When on his deathbed
he finally agreed to sell to Harris, assuring him that he
was free to do so, he told Ross: 'Frank has deprived
me of my only source of income by taking a play on
which I could always have raised £100.' (*L* 847)

In 1900 Ross arranged for Wilde to go to Rome.
He was seriously contemplating becoming a Catholic,
'though I fear that if I went before the Holy Father
with a blossoming rod it would turn at once into an
umbrella or something dreadful of that kind' (*L* 819).

On several occasions he attended papal audiences without result, but both in Rome and Palermo, where he stayed for a week, he was also pursuing cheap love — 'my mouth is twisted with kissing' (*L* 828) — Manuele, Francesco, Salvatore, Guiseppe ('whose eyes are beautiful. . . . Every day I kissed him behind the high altar': *L* 821), Arnoldo, Armando, Dario, Philippo (whom he picked up in the Vatican Palace). All these new affairs he faithfully reported to Ross, commenting: 'How evil it is to buy love, and how evil to sell it!' (*L* 828)

In his final year there was little in Wilde's life except misery. The tone of his letters is morbid, grasping, remorseful, vindictive, desperate. There are a few notes of happiness, all of them tinged by fearful apprehension: 'I am so lonely and poor. What is the end to be?' (*Clark cat.* III 4) He once sent Ross a pathetic note of bitter-sweetness: 'I have fallen in love with you again. . . . Our Indian winter.' (*L* 825) He had hopes of realising the value of the remaining Irish property, Moytura (his since Willie's death in March 1899), but this was taken by creditors in his still undischarged bankruptcy.

He borrowed unashamedly, ending up as he began, looking for 'the genial £5', constantly bemoaning the shortage of money, 'the most sordid and hungry of wants. . . . I keep on building castles of fairy gold in the air; we Celts always do.' (*L* 666) The 'champion playboy', Shaw said, had become 'the supertrifler' (Mary Hyde 129). He once accosted Nellie Melba for money like a common street-beggar. 'For four days I have had no cigarettes, no money to buy them, or notepaper,' he complained. (*L* 676) 'It is proposed to leave me to die of starvation, or to blow my brains out in a Naples urinal' (*L* 686); 'Neither to myself nor to others am I a joy. I am now simply an ordinary pauper of a rather low order' (*L* 695); 'I am going

under; the morgue yawns for me. . . . I had a wonderful life which is, I fear, over.' (*L* 708). A few friends
took him out for drinks. His addiction to absinthe,
the cheapest way to intoxication, increased, and his
conversation became coarse and consummately
cynical. As Shaw said later to Douglas, 'He went to
the devil his own way in spite of everybody . . . an
attempt to live on alcohol for the sake of the extraordinary power it gave him as an actor.' (Mary Hyde
59, 121) He was most often at the mercy of street-
arabs and the pseudo-poets — 'the noble army of the
Boulevard' (*L* 773). Richard Best and Synge saw him
at his time (*IR* 440), and Toulouse-Lautrec made
several telling sketches. He visited the Paris Exhibition of 1900, where he is believed to have recorded
some stanzas of *The Ballad of Reading Gaol* on an
Edison cylinder,[33] but he thought that he aroused
Parisian hostility by frightening away English visitors.
He joked that he would never outlive the century,
'as the English people could not stand him any more'
(Rothenstein 363). When an old boy-friend, Harry
Melvill, cut him, Wilde retorted: 'For people whom
one has had, to give themselves moral or social airs
is childish.' (*L* 760)

Wilde lived in the Hôtel d'Alsace, where the proprietor allowed him to accumulate a sizeable debt ('I
am dying beyond my means'), even paying the
medical expenses which now became necessary. In
prison Wilde had fallen, injuring his ear, and a suspected abscess developed. In 1898 he seems to have
had an operation on his throat, and also in a driving
accident he was thrown through the front window of
a fiacre. From February 1900 he was seriously ill,
and even allowing for his natural exaggeration there is
a note of panic in his letters as he observed the onset
of neurasthenia. Drink and sex were destroying the
fibre already psychologically and physically weakened

by prison, disgrace and early dissipation. On 10 October he had an operation on his ear and was [131] mostly confined to his room, where the British Embassy doctor made sixty-eight visits. He was unaware that Douglas, having left Paris in August, had secretly returned and had been roughed up while soliciting on the boulevards.[34]

It seems clear that Wilde was suffering from either neuro-syphilis or intracranial otitic sepsis, probably the latter.[35] In the last days of November it was obvious that he was dying, and he actually became delirious, then comatose. Ross and Turner were with him. Ross afterwards explained that he 'had always promised to bring a priest to Oscar when he was dying', adding: 'I felt rather guilty that I had so often dissuaded him from becoming a Catholic, but you know my reasons for doing so' (*L* 854) — this being a reference to his doubts as to Wilde's sincerity ('He was never quite sure himself where and when he was serious'). They fetched a priest, a Dublin-born Passionist Father, who, satisfied that Wilde was capable of response, administered conditional baptism, extreme unction and absolution.

Wilde died on 30 November 1900. Douglas arrived in time for the burial, which took place in the cemetery of Bagneux on 3 December.

4
Catharsis

1
An Author in Bankruptcy

The year 1900 was a psychological point of reference. Yeats said: 'In 1900 everybody got down off his stilts; henceforth nobody drank absinthe . . . nobody went mad; nobody committed suicide . . . nobody joined the Catholic Church.' (Hone 181) There was an immediate reaction to the 'Oscar Wilde affair' which gave him a life after death: besides the exodus to France of those who might have been under police surveillance, an 'athletic' tendency developed among English writers — beer-drinking, cricket-playing, Sussex-Downs-walking poets, figures such as Masefield, Squire, Belloc and Brooke.

On one side Wilde was regarded as equal to the Marquis de Sade and Gilles de Retz (*L* 431, 456): in 1913 E. M Forster's 'Maurice', to explain his condition, is forced to blurt out to an otherwise uncomprehending doctor: 'I am an unspeakable of the Oscar Wilde sort.' (Forster 139) On another side he was viewed as the English Verlaine or Dreyfus: 'a man who keeps an invulnerable innocence in spite of the habits of evil and misfortune', as Borges saw him (*TCV* 174). Contemporary verdicts on Wilde's trials varied: Richard Garnett, among those prophesying complete eclipse for the cause not only of sexual freedom but of artistic development, announced: 'That means the death of English poetry for fifty years' (Ford 77), and Watts-Dunton said the 'harlequin Wilde' had given the *coup de grâce* to the aesthetic movement (Rothenstein 232). Others like Dalhousie Young believed that 'Even if we know . . . what a man has done, we know nothing about the motive or the manner; and under the circumstances any outside judgement is a mere impertinence.' (Young 45) Lytton Strachey in 1921 believed that had the 'earthquake' not occurred, 'the history of English culture might have been quite different (Holroyd 828). 'Had he not scared the British public', said Gerhardie, 'by elevating his homosexual pseudo-paradise into a philosophy of life, but merely taunted them, like Shaw, with their social hypocrisy, he would have in the end earned their respect.' (Gerhardie 78) The 'affair' had been touch and go at all stages: a chance that Constance would divorce him; a chance that Queensberry could ignite Wilde's vanity into prosecution; a chance that once prosecuted he might abscond while on bail; a chance that he would be acquitted. At every point the alternative was an extreme — exculpation or damnation.

Already in 1895 a shutter had come down on Cyril and Vyvyan. Renamed Holland (a maternal family name), they were told to forget their background. Shortly before her death Constance wrote to Vyvyan:

> Try not to feel harshly about your father; remember that he is your father and that he loves you. All his troubles arose from the hatred of a son for his father, and whatever he has done he has suffered bitterly for. (*Son* 114)

After her death her family completely appropriated the boys, maintaining them incommunicado from their father, his friends and associates. On Wilde's death Ross succeeded in communicating with Cyril, then aged fifteen, who replied:

> I am glad you say he loved us. I hope that at his death he was truly penitent. . . . I only hope it will be a lesson for me and prevent me from falling into the snares and pitfalls of this world. (*Son* 134)

In 1914, at the age of twenty-nine, Cyril told his brother:

[134] I became obsessed with the idea that I must retrieve what had been lost. . . . All these years my great incentive has been to wipe that stain away; to retrieve, if may be, by some action of mine, a name no longer honoured in the land. . . . First and foremost, I must be a *man*. There was to be no cry of decadent artist, of effeminate aesthete, of weak-kneed degenerate. . . . I was no wild, passionate, irresponsible hero. I live by thought, not by emotion. I ask nothing better than to end in honourable battle for my King and Country. (*Son* 122: and so he did, in 1915 in France).

Vyvyan in fact remained ignorant of Ross's existence until 1907, and until 1905 was unaware of the cause of his father's disgrace, fearing that he had been a burglar or embezzler or bigamist, his greatest anxiety being that he and Cyril were illegitimate. Regarding his family's attitude he said: 'I do not altogether blame [them]. Even before the catastrophe they had all heartily disliked him, because he represented everything of which they fundamentally disapproved.' (*Son* 145) Until 1918 Vyvyan did not know his uncle Willie had left a daughter, Dorothy Ierne (Dolly) Wilde. (She seems to have inherited the family wit: told that she was fatter, she replied: 'It must be requited love'; a close friend of the Parisian lesbian Natalie Barney, she died in 1941.) The change of name was so effective that at university Vyvyan successfully concealed his true identity from even his closest friends such as Ronald Firbank. It was in 1907 that Ross enabled him to read 'De Profundis' complete and so understand much of his father's past.

As Wilde's literary executor Robert Ross's main purpose in the years following Wilde's death was to reestablish his reputation through the further publication of his works. A secondary aim was to safeguard Cyril's and Vyvyan's inheritance by turning a bankrupt estate into a profitable concern. The main plank in the campaign was the publication in 1905 of a carefully edited version of 'De Profundis', all personal direct [135] mention of Douglas excluded.

Ross was also conforming with Wilde's own wishes, that his reputation be salvaged by means of this apologia:

> The psychological explanation of a course of conduct. . . . Some day the truth will have to be known; not necessarily in my lifetime or in Douglas's; but I am not prepared to sit in the grotesque pillory they put me into, for all time. . . . I don't defend my conduct. I explain it. . . . Also my mental development in prison, and the inevitable evolution of character and intellectual attitude towards life that has taken place. (*L* 512)

Publication of 'De Profundis' was a clever psychological step. Corresponding to Wilde's defence in court of Uranian love, it maintained an attitude without making any extraordinary claims for its author. It persuaded some of the more cautious inverts that Wilde might still be useful to them. Laurence Housman wrote to Ross:

> It is the *right* sort of book to come now in order to touch the hearts of men made cruel by ignorance of human nature and history. Its reception seems to me remarkable — unprophesiable five or six years ago. . . . I hope provision is made to publish the work complete after this generation's nerves are laid in dust. (*CH* 243)[36]

In addition to restoring some faith in Wilde as a champion of the homosexual cause, the publication of 'De Profundis' also led to the financial success of his other works, particularly the publication of his *Collected Works* in 1908 in fourteen volumes. In that year Ross was able to announce the final discharge of the Wilde estate from bankruptcy. At a dinner given in his honour in 1908 he said:

A kind-hearted official at the Court of Bankruptcy assured me in 1901, when the creditors had received about three shillings in the pound sterling, that Wilde's works were of no value, and would never command any interest whatever. It was a less hard successor who, with more enthusiasm, relieved me of the first £1,000 produced by *De Profundis*.

(*Ross* 154)

However, in 1897 Ross himself had seen no monetary value in *The Ballad of Reading Gaol* (see *L* 653), and he certainly did not have a wholesale regard for Wilde's work. For example, he said of *Vera*:

This play is such damned nonsense that I have purposely left it out of the 5/- or 1/- editions. I really could not allow it to be accessible. Wilde was only 21 when he wrote it. . . . However if there is money in the film rights of course we must submit, *but there must be no further publication of the text.* . . . I never could find out what the plot was: it was very clever of you to invent one.[37]

Although by 1906 the English creditors had been paid in full, mainly from productions of Wilde's plays in Germany and the early proceeds from 'De Profundis', Ross's difficulties increased, largely owing to the vindictive attitude of Douglas, who had refused Ross's offer of a half-share in the estate and who called Ross 'the High Priest of all the Sodomites in London . . . a filthy bugger, a notorious sodomite, an habitual debaucher and corruptor of young boys, and a black-mailer' (*Autobiography* 423). Such harrying, reminiscent of Queensberry, contributed to Ross's own public disgrace and his early death in 1918. It also caused him, for the effect of annoying Douglas, to insist that posters for Wilde's plays over which he had control should state 'By permission of the

Author's Literary Executor Robert Ross'.

Probably one of Ross's most fortunate and intelligent steps was to realise the coming importance of film, on which much of Vyvyan Holland's later prosperity was to rest:

It has always occurred to me that many of Wilde's stories would make much better Kinema films than the actual plays — I refer particularly to 'The Young King' and 'The Birthday of the Infanta', which, as you know, have been made into ballets in Russia and, I think, in Germany. . . . I presume some kind of words, however foolish, would have to be composed for the actors who play in front of the camera.

A further act of piety on Ross's part was to enable a tomb — much more than a simple monument — to be commissioned from the controversial young sculptor Epstein. This was completed in 1912 and placed, after some objections from the authorities, in the Père Lachaise cemetery, to which Wilde's remains had been transferred in 1909. Ross's ashes are also in the tomb.

2
'We All Need Masks'

With the encouragement of the acclaim following the publication of the collected edition in 1908, serious interest began to be directed towards Wilde. With the scrutiny of Strachey, Forster, the Sitwells, Cyril Connolly, Auden and Eliot, a 'modern' view began to be formed, bringing him into a twentieth-century perspective. Symons, reviewing the *Collected Works* brought out the fact that Wilde's reputation was fragmented:

Such an artificial world Wilde created. . . . In Germany he is the author of 'Salome', in France a poet and critic, in England the creator of 'The Ballad of Reading Gaol' or perhaps of 'De Profundis'. Nowhere is there any agreement as to the question of relative merit; in fact, nowhere is there any due acknowledgement of what the merit really is. There is, indeed, so much variety in Wilde's work, he has made so many experiments in so many directions, that it is only now . . . that we can trace the curious movement, forward and backward, of a mind never fully certain of its direction. (*CH* 294-5)

Perhaps the real meaning of Wilde's statement to Gide was that it required genius to live such a life as he conceived his to be — the real work of art. Certainly this is what Yeats understood when he admired Wilde's living a mythology he had invented for himself: he was not so much attempting to *be* a poet, but posing *as* a poet; not so much pursuing a career as a critic, but posing in a critical stance. In 'real life' he was too polished in manners to be a gentleman, too effusive to be a friend, too precocious to love or hate. Wilde's posthumous reputation rests on two apparently irreconcilable elements: firstly, that his critics and admirers, including Klee, Kandinsky, Mann, Gide, Picasso, Nabokov and Barthes (cf. Chamberlin 20, 40, 191), took him seriously even when they knew him to be insincere; secondly, that as a man famous for his piquant wit, he generated a new relationship of joker to subject. In the first category he appears as cynic, symbolist, decadent; in the second as farceur, poseur, blagueur. In fact there is no demarcation between the two: the levity of the dandy spills into the critical path of the decadent man of letters. Thus it was possible for Joyce, a self-made exile and outsider, to see Wilde in the tradition of Irish dramatists playing 'court jester to the English' (see *TCV* 58) and for Auden to call him a typical modern outsider (see

TCV 116-17); he was 'one of the last romantics' and a forerunner of the drama of alienation; both Yeats and Beckett are affected by his 'truth of masks'; while Beaton, in the continuing 'farce' of aestheticism, proved that the camera *can* lie.

It was natural for Vyvyan's friend Firbank to imitate Wilde in producing dandiacal works which he took a step further by liberating from nineteenth-century form. Still bound by that form, Beerbohm's 'Happy Hypocrite', based on *Dorian Gray*, appeared in Wilde's lifetime (see *L* 576), while Harold Acton, perhaps the last of the great Victorians, produced 'La Belle au Bois Dormant' under the influence of 'The Harlot's House'. The disdainful attitude of the dandy who, as Cyril Connolly said, 'disliked the bourgeoisie, idealised the aristocracy, and treated the lower classes as his brothel' (Connolly 46) rings true of both Wilde and Firbank and, one suspects, of many figures in 'Bloomsbury'.

Wilde's direct influence on behaviour can also be traced. A. J. A. Symons remarked:

> I myself have been in debt ever since I reached the age of discretion. To be in debt, in fact, is one of the plainest signs that the age of discretion has been attained, and those who are monotonously solvent have probably never fully grown up. (*Book Collector* III no. 3).

However, a collaborator in Queensberry's witch-hunt later recalled:

> Wilde will always have his sympathisers; but not among those who . . . knew the misery he was causing in many homes and the bad influence which survived his disappearance. (*IR* 289)

The destruction of English domesticity, the intellectual corruption of British youth, was one offence. 'The fact of a man being a poisoner', says

Wilde, 'is nothing against his prose.' (*W* 1007) A recent
[140] view from Monk Gibbon helps to place Wilde in the
perspective of emancipation from Pre-Raphaelite to
'angry young man':

> I admire Wilde as a poet and wit and am ready to
> believe that he was gentle, clean-spoken and a
> romanticist in his own aberrative way. On the other
> hand I think his declaration of war on the Non-
> conformist conscience was carried so far in certain
> of his essays [that] he helped to destroy utterly
> the characteristic puritanical Englishman and to
> produce instead the present-day sniggering, emancip-
> ated, essentially adolescent, self-supposedly-daring
> English 'intellectual' whom I despise and abhor.[38]

There is something of this latter intellect in the pseudo-
aestheticism so detested by *Punch* — destroying the
seriousness of English art and manners.

Cyril Connolly analysed the homosexual writer's
equipment as 'combativeness, curiosity, egotism,
intuition and adaptability' (Connolly 125). There was
a stream of consciousness in Wilde, discernible in his
letters, poems, essays, plays and conduct, which *com-
bated* the world — its roles, its behaviour, its logic,
reality itself; another which shows us his *curiosity* for
'strange passions' or sensations of eye, ear, taste and
intellect; another displaying his feminine *intuition* —
the critical ability to see the correspondence between
different matrices; while his *adaptability* is evident in
every turn and twist of his philosophy, making it
almost impossible for the literalist to pin down his
butterfly thoughts.[39] But the characteristics which
emerge most forcibly from Wilde's case history are his
egotism, his extroversion, his theatricality, his attitudinising, his self-dramatisation; and his strongest weapon
was his array of masks to conceal himself from himself
as much as from the world. This places Wilde firmly in

the tradition — to look no further back — from Baudelaire (see Starkie 116) to Eliot ('to prepare a face to meet the faces that you meet'). Is there also a line of descent from Baudelaire's 'hypocrite lecteur' through Wilde's *Dorian Gray*, to Eliot's *The Waste Land*?; or from Baudelaire's 'In decadence dandyism is the last outburst of heroism', through Wilde's hermaphrodite dandyism to Eliot's Prufrock: 'Shall I part my hair behind? Do I dare to eat a peach? . . . Do I dare disturb the universe?'?

There seem to have been three Oscar Wildes, corresponding to those in *Dorian Gray*: firstly, the artist contemplating, reproducing, and dominated by, the creature of beauty — as Wilde conceived himself; secondly, the hedonist, acknowledging neither right nor wrong in his pursuit and propagation of pleasure — thus the world saw Wilde; thirdly, the thing of beauty itself, living in a world of Hellenic purity, unconscious of guilt.[40] He had, in the five years which culminated in his appearances at the Old Bailey, committed offences in writing, speech and behaviour contrary to Victorian ethics; he had done it with advertisement, and then denied that he had done it. As he said of Wainewright the poisoner, 'A publicist, nowadays, is a man who bores the community with the details of the illegality of his private life.' (*W* 1102)

Wilde typified 'genius wedded to insanity' (*CH* 132), the interaction of the 'Regency' and the Gothic tradition on which the aesthetic movement fed so hungrily. It was the reservoir of his extraordinary courage and his capacity for despair, his vanity turning to recklessness, and his heraldic insistence on the free play of mind; and it explains how, imaginatively rooted in an age fifty years before his own, he could also be so modern, dandy of manner, dandy of wit, dandy of morals — 'a problem for which there was no solution' (*L* 685).

Notes

1 Laurence Housman, *Echo de Paris* (1923): a composite portrait of Wilde in his last years, and not therefore an authentic quotation.

2 Speranza's *Poems* (1864) were dedicated 'to my sons Willie and Oscar Wilde'. Her final poem, 'Moral', reads ironically:

> God give us grace, each in his place / To keep from sin and sinning: / Our souls we sell for gifts from Hell / That are not worth the winning . . . / False fruit that turns to ashes.

3 Rossetti, Scott, Byron, Hugo, Vigny, Balzac and Baudelaire all recorded their indebtedness to *Melmoth*. Balzac wrote a sequel, *Melmoth reconcilié à l'église*.

4 There had, of course, been earlier germs: Ruskin's *Pre-Raphaelitism* appeared in 1851, Darwin's *Origin of Species*, Smiles's *Self-Help* and Mill's *Essay on Liberty* in 1859; but the appearance of such pioneering works as Swinburne's *Poems and Ballads* (1866), Arnold's *Culture and Anarchy* (1869), Tylor's *Primitive Culture* (1871), Pater's *Renaissance* (1873), Symonds's translation of Michelango's *Sonnets* (1878), two series of Symonds's *Studies in the Greek Poets* (1873 and 1876), Mahaffy's *Social Life in Greece* (1874) and Renan's *Dialogues Philosophiques* (1876, thirteen years after his revolutionary *La Vie de Jésus*) laid the foundation on which the 1880s – in which Wilde came into his own – could discuss aesthetic issues.

5 M. Critchley, *Medico-Legal Journal*, XXX, no. 2 (1962), 79.

6 The Oxford Union approved a motion welcoming 'the efforts being made to bring Art and Literature within reach of the masses of Englishmen' but condemning 'the ridiculous class known as aesthetes' (Chamberlin 73). It is in fact the editor of *Punch*, F. C. Burnand, who is credited by the *Oxford English Dictionary* with coining the word 'aesthetic' in his satire *The Colonel*. The *OED* defines the

word as 'one who professes a superior appreciation of what is beautiful, and endeavours to carry out his ideas in practice'. *Punch* referred (28 May 1881) to the pseudo-aesthetes' 'richly sentimental paganism'.

7   It is said that Willie failed at the Irish Bar and therefore sought a career in Fleet Street, but although he is commonly dismissed as a drunken womaniser, he was also a writer and talker of considerable ability. As one witness affirms, he was

> a very distinct personality in London for many years . . . the supreme type of the cultured journalist. . . . Nothing like Willie Wilde's work had ever been done before in journalism. It was absolutely sane. There was nothing of the affectation, no hint or trace of the paradox or the epigrams employed by Oscar. . . . In his own fashion his talk was as memorable as his brother's. It did not astonish so much as it charmed. When Oscar Wilde talked one went away with a brain full of new ideas, many of which one felt were in some sort reprehensible. . . . When Willie Wilde had talked to you for an hour or two you always went away chuckling with pleasure, rather than stumbling in mental amazement.

Years later Max Beerbohm contrasted the brothers rather differently:

> Oscar Luxury — gold-tipped matches — hair curled — Assyrian — . . . not soigné . . . cat-like tread — heavy shoulders — enormous dowager — . . . jollity overdone — But real ability. Willie: quel monstre! Dark, oily, suspect yet awfully like Oscar: he has Oscar's coy sensual smile and fatuous giggle, and not a little of Oscar's aspect. But he is awful — a veritable tragedy of family likeness. (White 244)

In fact Willie became not only a successful gossip columnist and drama critic but also a leader-writer and reporter — his coverage of the Parnell Commission in 1888-89 was particularly commended. Shaw, however called him 'a vulgar journalist of no account' (*IR* 408).

8   750 copies of *Poems* were printed, to be used in three equal editions (June, July and September 1881). A further 500 copies were printed in 1882 for the fourth and fifth editions, of which by 1892 over 200 copies remained unsold.

9   This is a clear reference to the perplexity of Saul and Jonathan: 'I did but taste a little honey with the end of the rod that was in mine hand, and, lo, I must die' (1 Samuel 14: 43), also quoted by Pater in his essay on the eighteenth-century homosexual Winckelmann.

10 On 'Uranian' poetry see d'Arch Smith *Love in Earnest* (1970). The word 'Uranian' which (occurs in Wilde's *Letters*, 705) was coined by K. M. Ulrichs to express the kind of love which follows the 'higher philosophy' of Plato's *Symposium*. See Havelock Ellis, *Sexual Inversion* (1936).

11 The penalty for 'buggery', i.e. sodomy (with humans) or bestiality (with animals), under Section 61 of the Offences Against the Person Act, 1861, was penal servitude for life. The law remained in force until 1892. Previously the penalty had been death.

12 It was actually performed, under the title 'Guido Ferranti' and without the author's name on the playbills, in New York from 21 January until 14 February 1891. Wilde seems scarcely justified in claiming that it was 'an immense success and excited much curiosity' (*L* 283). An invitation to Irving to produce it in London at that time was declined.

13 Contributors included Princess Christian, 'Carmen Sylva' (i.e. the Queen of Roumania), the Countesses of Munster, Shrewsbury, Meath, Portsmouth and Cork, Lady Dorothy Nevill, Lady Archibald Campbell, Olive Schreiner, 'Violet Fane' (i.e. Mary Lamb, soon to be Lady Currie), 'Marie Corelli', Anne Ritchie Thackeray, 'George Fleming' (i.e. Julia Fletcher), 'Ouida', Helena Sickert, Mathilde Blind, Arthur Symons and the Uranians Gleeson White and Oscar Browning.

14 *The Happy Prince and other tales* contained four pieces in addition to the title story: 'The Nightingale and the Rose', 'The Selfish Giant', 'The Devoted Friend' and 'The Remarkable Rocket'.

15 Particular attention should be given to a comparison of Wilde's dialogue with Paget/Lee's *Belcaro*, 'A Dialogue on Poetic Morality' (1881), 246-7, 252, 263, where, ten years ahead of *Dorian Gray*, she predicts the development of aestheticism into decadence.

16 This is given in Hyde 107 and *Son* 45 as 'Atha me in mu codladh is/agus na duishe me', which is inaccurate: I have taken the line from Brian Tobin, who heard it from Vyvyan Holland, and wrote it in the Connaught Irish which Wilde would most likely have heard in Leenane or Cong.

17 Vyvyan Holland recalled the golf-clubs standing in the hall at Tite Street — Ross assured him they had been used [145] inefficiently but enthusiastically by Wilde (*Son* 175).

18 *A House of Pomegranates* contained 'The Young King' (1888), 'The Star Child', 'The Fisherman and his Soul' and 'The Birthday of the Infanta' (1889). *Lord Arthur Savile's Crime and other stories* contained, besides the title story, 'The Sphinx Without a Secret' (1887, as 'Lady Alroy'), 'The Canterville Ghost' (1887) and 'The Model Millionaire' (1887).

19 See A. Storr, *The Dynamics of Creation* (1972 and 1976), 51, 241. Perhaps Wilde's feverish activity explains what Joyce called 'the epileptic tendency of his nervous system' (*TCV* 59).

20. The names of Michelangelo, Shakespeare and Winckelmann occur frequently as 'honourable' or 'exceptional' examples of homosexuality in the arts. Symonds's translation of Michelangelo's sonnets (1878) had given an impetus to the production of Uranian verse in England. Winckelmann was the subject of a notable essay by Pater (1867; repr. 1873).

21 Wilde was 'Menalcas' in Gide's *Fruits of the Earth (Les Nourritures Terrestres*, 1897) and also appeared in *L'Immoraliste* (1902) and is discussed in *If It Die (Si le Grain ne Meurt*, 1920-21) and *Corydon* (1911). In the latter Gide admired Wilde's consistency in upholding his beliefs: 'To try to establish one's innocence by disavowing one's life is to yield to public opinion.'

22 It is important for Wilde's relevance outside the field of English letters to note that the first performance of *Salome* (in French) was given at the pioneering Théâtre de l'Oeuvre of Lugné-Poë in Paris in 1896 while Wilde was in Reading prison ('It is something that at a time of disgrace and shame I should still be regarded as an artist': *L 399)* and that it was subsequently presented by Max Reinhardt at his Kleines Theater, Berlin, in 1902 and at many other private theatres before its first public performance in the British Isles at the Peacock Theatre, Dublin, by the Dublin Gate Theatre Studio, produced by Hilton Edwards and designed by Micheál Mac Liammóir in 1928.

23 Wilde and Shaw, close contemporaries, were not collaborators, but had a mild flirtation as the progenitors of 'the great Celtic school' (*L* 339). 'England is the land of intellectual fogs but you have done much to clear the air,' Wilde wrote. 'We are both Celtic and I like to think

that we are friends.' (*L* 332) Opus 1 was *Lady Windermere's Fan*; Opus 2 *Widowers' Houses*, the preface to which Wilde called 'a real masterpiece of trenchant writing and caustic wit and dramatic instinct' (*L* 339); Opus 3 was *A Woman of No Importance*; Opus 4 *The Philanderer*; Opus 5 *An Ideal Husband*. As Hesketh Pearson observed, 'Wilde thus paid Shaw the compliment of ranking their works together in the dramatic literature of the age, though he had just scored his second huge success . . . while Shaw had practically been hooted from the stage.' (Pearson, *GBS* 132) Shaw 'always made a point of treating Wilde with great respect as a serious writer' as he later told Douglas: 'We were Irishmen, resenting strongly the English practice of making pets of Irishmen. We understood one another on this point, and thereby made our relationship quite unintelligible in England.' (Mary Hyde 36-7)

24 Mary McCarthy points out that 'Depravity is the hero and the only character. . . . The title is a blague.' (*TCV* 108) Shaw called it 'a soulless farce without a single human being or human moment in it' (Mary Hyde 128).

25 In 1887 Wilde had suggested to 'Violet Fane' that she write an essay on 'The Demoralising Influence of Nature': 'It is those who live in the country whom Nature deteriorates.' (*L* 207)

26 Although the card was reproduced in the original edition of *Trials* and on the endpaper of Hyde, it has only once been quoted correctly (Stokes); others fill out the accusation 'For Oscar Wilde, posing *as a* sodomite', thus slightly changing the meaning; even Hyde himself misquotes it (p. 196), as he does in *Trials* (p. 76). Mary Hyde asserts that Queensberry took legal advice before using this form of words (p.xv).

27 Harris's account of the 'strange exodus' (pp. 250-1), in which 'every train to Dover was crowded, every steamer to Calais thronged with members of the aristocratic and leisured classes', is, of course, exaggerated, but it is true that several key figures did go abroad. Ross, Turner and Douglas all went to France for safety, Douglas remaining abroad for three years, while many others who might have been under police surveillance took temporary refuge in Dieppe or Calais.

28 Starting from a slightly lower status in the Dublin professional class (his father was an architect and, as with Wilde, his two uncles were clergymen), Carson had follow-

ed a successful legal career which made him Solicitor-General for Ireland and, in 1892, MP for Dublin University as a Liberal Unionist, a political grouping Wilde had satirised in *The Importance of Being Earnest*. He was the first Irish QC to take silk at the English Bar, where he had been practising only since 1893.

29 I was told this by the late Micheál Mac Liammóir who heard it, I believe, from Vyvyan Holland, who heard it from a member of the Carson family.

30 However, Douglas maintained to the end of his life that he should have been called to discredit his father, and he once told Shaw (in 1938) that Clarke had in fact agreed to call him (Mary Hyde 90).

31 Section 11 of the Criminal Law Amendment Act, 1885, read:

> *Outrages on decency*: Any male person who, in public or private, commits, or is a party to the commission of, or procures or attempts to procure the commission by any male person of any act of gross indecency with another male person, shall be guilty of a misdemeanour, and being convicted thereof shall be liable at the discretion of the court to be imprisoned for any term not exceeding two years, with or without hard labour.

32 Wilde gave Ross the manuscript of 'De Profundis', which he had earlier instructed him to have typed and the original sent to Douglas. It is not certain that Ross carried out these instructions: from Douglas's subsequent behaviour it seems highly improbable that he had seen this catalogue of his faults as a person and a lover, whereas Wilde appears to have assumed that Douglas had read it. Ross subsequently published a suitably edited version in 1905, but Douglas claimed that his first knowledge of the real import of the letter was when the whole document was disclosed in the course of a court action in 1913. The mystery is, I believe, solved by Ross's inscription in one copy of the text:

> The MS never passed into his [i.e. Douglas's] possession. He received a copy of it in Wilde's lifetime, on 9 August 1897. But he denied this. . . . I can prove his perjury by his own letters to me and Sir George Lewis, and the independent evidence of common friends. (*Clark cat.* II 90)

There is no reason for Ross to have falsified this: delivery of 'De Profundis' to Douglas would have forced the lovers apart (which Ross the jealous boyfriend wanted) rather than throwing them back into one another's arms.

33 I have listened carefully to the Edison recording and am

convinced that it is nowadays played at the wrong speed –
distorting the mezzo voice which Beerbohm remembered.

34 *Le Journal* reported that Douglas was 'well-known on the
boulevards, a gentleman who practices in his own way
"Suffer the little children to come unto me"' (d'Arch
Smith 48-50).

35 T. Cawthorne, 'The Last Illness of Oscar Wilde', *Proceedings of The Royal Society of Medicine*, LII, no. 2 (1959)
123-7, agrees with Critchley (source quoted in note 5),
although the latter in *Med. Hist.*, I (1957), 149, alleges that
an undergraduate poem by Wilde, dedicated to an Oxford
prostitute, from whom it has often been said (e.g. by Sherard)
that he contracted syphilis, has been discovered, 'hinting at
an intimate and disastrous association'. Cawthorne agrees
that syphilis is an obvious cause of nerve deafness and that
it may also have been responsible for a rash Wilde had
earlier that year (from supposed mussel poisoning), but this
could also have been due to dermititis secondary to
vitamin deficiency. 'If he had suffered from uncomplicated
leptomeningitis, then delirium sufficiently mild to have
been noteworthy would have preceded the final coma.
Thus it seems likely that he had a temporal lobe abcess in
the dominant hemisphere secondary to chronic suppurative
otitis media.' Cawthorne concludes that 'His habits and
way of life played little part in his early demise.'

36 The complete publication came in 1949 (in an inaccurate
version) in *Works* (pp. 873-957) and in 1962 in *Letters*
(pp. 423-511).

37 This, like other papers quoted here, forms part of a collection relating to the literary estate of Oscar Wilde which I
was permitted to examine by the senior partner of Parker,
Garrett & Co. (formerly Parker, Garrett & Holman), Ross's
solicitors and subsequently Vyvyan Holland's. It is an
extensive record of the Wilde literary estate, including a
previously unpublished letter by Wilde to Tree relating to
the rights in *A Woman of No Importance*.

38 In a letter dated 6 November 1968.

39 Henry James commented: 'Everything Oscar does is a deliberate trap for the literalist, and to see the literalist walk
straight up to it, look straight at it, and step straight into
it, makes one freshly avert a discouraged gaze from this
unspeakable animal.' (Edel II 39)

40 As Shaw observed, 'guilty or not guilty is a question not
of fact but of morals' and Wilde could 'plead not guilty
with perfect sincerity, and indeed could not honestly put
in any other plea' (Mary Hyde 80).

Bibliography

The following are referred to in the text. The list is not exhaustive (as is E. H. Mikhail's *Bibliography*), and books referred to in the Abbreviations section (p. 4) are not repeated here.

All the following books and periodicals were published in London unless otherwise stated.

An excellent reading list is also contained in Stokes (see below), and an account of the primary sources is given in Hyde.

Archer, Charles, *William Archer: Life, and Frienships*, New Haven, Conn., 1931

Beerbohm, Max, *A Peep into the Past*, 1923; repr. 1972

Beerbohm, Max, *Letters to Reggie Turner*, ed. Rupert Hart-Davis, 1964

Bendz, Ernest, *Oscar Wilde: A Retrospect*, Folcroft, Penn., 1969

Benson, E. F., *As We Were: A Victorian Peep-Show*, 1930

Benson, E. F., *Final Edition: An Informal Autobiography*, 1940

Blair, Sir David Hunter, *In Victorian Days*, 1939

Brasol, Boris, *Oscar Wilde: The Man, the Artist, the Martyr*, 1938 (contains useful chronology)

Broad, Lewis, *The Friendships and Follies of Oscar Wilde*, 1954; repr. (pb) as *The Truth About Oscar Wilde*, 1957

Brown, R. D., '*Suetonius, Symonds and Gibbon in The Picture of Dorian Gray*', *Modern Language Notes*, Baltimore, Md., LXXI (1956)

Camus, Albert, *The Rebel (L'Homme Revolté*, trans. Anthony Bower), 1962

Carpenter, Edward, *Defence of Criminals*, 1889

Carpenter, Edward, *Towards Democracy*, 1883; repr. 1885, 1892

Carpenter, Edward, *Love's Coming-of-Age* [1895]; repr. 1896

Cawthorne, Terence, 'The Last Illness of Oscar Wilde', *Proceedings of the Royal Society of Medicine*, LII, no. 2 (1959)

Cecil, Lord David, *Max: A Biography*, 1964 [Max Beerbohm]

Chamberlin, J. E., *Ripe Was the Drowsy Hour: The Age of
[150]   Oscar Wilde*, New York, 1977
'Cheiro' [Count Louis Hamon], *Cheiro's Memoirs: The
   Reminiscences of a Society Palmist*, 1912
Connell, John, *W. E. Henley*, 1949
Connolly, Cyril, *Enemies of Promise*, 1938; repr. (pb) 1961
Critchley, Macdonald, 'Medical Reflections on Oscar Wilde',
   Medico-Legal Journal, Cambridge, XXX (1962)
Critchley, Macdonald, *Med. Hist.*, I (1957)
Croft-Cooke, Rupert, *The Unrecorded Life of Oscar Wilde*,
   1972
Croft-Cooke, Rupert, *Feasting With Panthers: A New Con-
   sideration of Some Late Victorian Writers*, 1967
d'Arch Smith, Timothy, *Love in Earnest*, 1970 (excellent
   bibliography of Uranian literature, 1860-1930)
de Goncourt, Edmond, *The Goncourt Journal (Journal des
   Goncourts*, trans. R. Baldick), Oxford, 1962
Douglas, Lord Alfred, *Without Apology*, 1938
Douglas, Lord Alfred, *Autobiography*, 1929
Edel, Leon, *The Life of Henry James*, 6 vols, 1953-72
Ellis, Havelock, *Sexual Inversion*, 1897
Ellis, Havelock, *Studies in the Psychology of Sex*, 4 vols, 1936
Ellmann, Richard, *Eminent Domain: Yeats among Wilde,
   Joyce, Pound, Eliot and Auden*, Oxford, 1967
Ford, Ford Madox, *Memories and Impressions*, ed. M. Killigrew
   1971; repr. (pb) 1979
Forster, E. M., *Maurice* [1913-14], 1971
Furniss, Harry, *Some Victorian Women*, 1923
Gerhardie, William, *God's Fifth Column: A Biography of the
   Age: 1890-1940*, ed. Michael Holroyd and Robert Skidelsky,
   1981
Gide, André, *If It Die (Si le Grain ne Meurt*, trans. D. Bussy),
   1951
Gide, André, *Fruits of the Earth (Les Nourritures Terrestres)*,
   1949; repr. (pb) 1970
Gide, André, *The Immoralist (L'Immoraliste)*, 1902
Gide, André, *Corydon*, 1911
Gunn, Peter, *Vernon Lee: Violet Paget, 1856-1935*, 1964
Hamilton, Walter, *The Aesthetic Movement in England*, 1882
Harris, Frank, *Oscar Wilde: His Life and Confessions*, 2 vols,
   New York, 1918
Holland, Vyvyan [Vyvyan Wilde], *Son of Oscar Wilde*, 1954;
   repr. (pb) 1957
Holroyd, Michael, *Lytton Strachey; A Biography*, revised ed.
   (pb) 1971

Hone, Joseph, *W. B. Yeats*, 1943; repr. (pb) 1971

Hough, Graham, *The Last Romantics*, 1949 [151]

Housman, Laurence, *Echo de Paris*, 1923

Huysmans, Joris-Karl, *Against Nature (A Rebours*, trans. R. Baldick), 1959

Hyde, Harford Montgomery, *Oscar Wilde: The Aftermath*, 1963

Hyde, Harford Montgomery, *The Cleveland Street Scandal*, 1976

Hyde, Mary, ed., *Bernard Shaw and Alfred Douglas: A Correspondence*, 1982

Jackson, Holbrook, *The Eighteen Nineties*, 1913; repr. (pb) 1939; New York, 1966; new illustrated ed. (intro. C. Campos) Brighton, 1976

James, Henry, *Letters of Henry James*, Vol. I, New York, 1929

Krafft-Ebbing, R. von, *Psychopathia Sexualis*, 12th ed., New York, 1965

Lee, Vernon [Violet Paget] *Belcaro*, 1881

Le Gallienne, Richard, *The Romantic 90s*, 1926

Levey, Michael, *The Case of Walter Pater*, 1978

Mahaffy, J. P., *Principles of the Art of Conversation*, 1887

Mahaffy, J. P., *Social Life in Greece from Homer to Menander*, 1874

Maturin, C.R., *Melmoth the Wanderer*, Edinburgh, 1820; repr. 1892; Oxford, 1968; (pb) 1977

Mikhail, E. H., *Oscar Wilde: An Annotated Bibliography of Criticism*, 1978

Morley, Sheridan, *Oscar Wilde: An Illustrated Biography*, 1976

Nordau, Max, *Degeneration*, 1895

O'Sullivan, Vincent, *Aspects of Wilde*, 1936

Pater, Walter, *Studies in the History of the Renaissance*, 1873

Pater, Walter, *Marius the Epicurean: His Sensations and Ideas*, 1885

Pearson, Hesketh, *Labby: The Life of Henry Labouchere*, 1936

Pearson, Hesketh, *GBS, A Postscript*, 1951

Raffalovich, André, *Uranisme et unisexualité*, Paris, 1896 [originally published as *L'Affaire Oscar Wilde*]

Rothenstein, William, *Men and Memories: 1872-1900*, 1931

Ruskin, John, *Pre-Raphaelitism*, 1851, repr. 1854

Savoy Operas, The, 1926

Sherard, Robert Harborough, *The Life of Oscar Wilde*, 1906

Shewan, Rodney, *Oscar Wilde: Art and Egotism*, 1977

[152]

Stanford, W. B., and McDowell, R.B., *Mahaffy*, 1971
Starkie, Enid, *Baudelaire*, 1957; repr. (pb) 1971
Stokes, John, *Oscar Wilde*, 1978
Storr, Anthony, *The Dynamics of Creation*, 1972; repr. 1976
Sullivan, Kevin, *Oscar Wilde*, 1972
Symonds, John Addington, *Studies in the Greek Poets: First Series*, 1873; *Second Series*, 1876
Symonds, John Addington, *A Problem in Greek Ethics*, Bristol, 1883
Symonds, John Addington, *A Problem in Modern Ethics*, Davos, 1891
Symonds, John Addington, trans. *The Sonnets of Michelangelo*, 1878
Symonds, John Addington, *Letters*, ed. H. M. Schueller and R. C. Peters, 2 vols, Detroit, 1967-68
Symons, A. J. A., *Essays and Biographies*, ed. Julian Symons, 1969
Symons, Arthur, *A Study of Oscar Wilde*, 1930
Tyrrell, R. Y., and Sullivan, Sir E., ed., *Echoes from 'Kottabos'*, 1906
White, Terence de Vere, *The Parents of Oscar Wilde*, 1967
Whistler, James MacNeill, *The Gentle Art of Making Enemies*, 1890
Whitman, Walt, *Leaves of Grass*, New York, 1855
Wilson, Colin, *The Outsider*, 1956, repr. (pb) 1963
Winwar, Frances [F. Grebanier], *Oscar Wilde and the Yellow Nineties*, 1940
Woodcock, George, *Anarchism*, 1963
Yeats, W. B., *Autobiographies*, 1955
Yeats, W. B., 'Introduction', *Oxford Book of Modern Verse*, Oxford, 1936
Yeats, W. B., *Fairy and Folk Tales*, 1889
Yeats, W. B., *The Wanderings of Oisin*, 1889
Young, Dalhousie, *Apologia pro Oscar Wilde*, 1895
Y.T.O. [L.C.M.S. Amery, F. W. Hirst, H. A. A. Cruso] *Aristophanes at Oxford: O.W.*, 1894

Index